POPE FRANCIS

POPE FRANCIS

Walking Together

The Way of Synodality

Maryknoll, New York 10545

Founded in 1970, Orbis Books endeavors to publish works that enlighten the mind, nourish the spirit, and challenge the conscience. The publishing arm of the Maryknoll Fathers and Brothers, Orbis seeks to explore the global dimensions of the Christian faith and mission, to invite dialogue with diverse cultures and religious traditions, and to serve the cause of reconciliation and peace. The books published reflect the views of their authors and do not represent the official position of the Maryknoll Society. To learn more about Maryknoll and Orbis Books, please visit our website at www.orbisbooks.com

---

English language edition published in 2023 by Orbis Books, Box 302, Maryknoll, NY 10545-0302.

English translations drawn from www.vatican.va.

Manufactured in the United States of America

ISBN 978-1-62698-524-7 (print)
ISBN 978-1-60833-985-3 (ebook)

Library of Congress Control Number: 2022038376

Contents

Preface

I am very pleased to present this collection of Pope Francis's interventions, edited by the General Secretariat of the Synod. Its merit is that of retracing the pope's words on the themes of the Synod and synodality, which are closely intertwined, weaving together, so to speak, a "red thread" that makes it possible to reconstruct, now almost ten years after the beginning of his pontificate, the accentuations and developments that those themes have so far known.

This is a text, in my opinion, that will be useful to many. It will be useful first of all to those faithful who, especially in the context of the current 2021–23 synodal process, wish to better understand what Pope Francis is thinking when he speaks of the synodal church; it was, after all, his magisterium that gave synodality an unprecedented and unquestioned centrality in the current journey of the church. But it will also be useful to those specialists interested in exploring the multiple theological implications of synodality, who will here find Pope Francis's main interventions at hand.

Without claiming to offer an exhaustive summary of the Holy Father's rich teaching on synodality, I limit myself below to suggesting three simple thematic focuses, which I hope will prove helpful to the reader.

The first focus is related to the theme of *discernment*. This is an exceptionally frequent term in the pope's magisterium. It is discernment that marks the fundamental difference between synodality and parliamentarianism. Synodality is not finding a compromise between divergent positions, as is customary (in a way that is in itself legitimate) in parliamentary chambers; synodality, rather, is getting together to listen to the Holy Spirit in order to reach an inner consensus on God's will here and now for his church. The insistence on listening and docility to the Spirit is so persevering that it is, in a sense, the defining feature of the pope's vision of synodality. Only a church skilled in the art of discernment, both personal and communal, is a church that does not merely "have" or "do" a synod, but one that learns to "be" a synod.

The second focus has to do with the *pastoral ministry.* A synodal church is a church that rediscovers the protagonism, theological and pastoral, of all the baptized, because all believers have received the anointing of the Spirit that makes the People of God infallible *in credendo*. This inevitably brings with it a profound rethinking in the way ordained ministry is conceived and exercised. The authority that derives from the sacrament of Holy Orders is but an empowerment to service: to the service of all the baptized, so that they may express their gifts and charisms for the growth of the church and thus contribute to the coming of the Kingdom. That authority is always exercised, Pope Francis affirms, within the People of God and for the People of God. It requires going beyond a clericalist vision that erects fences between pastors and the faithful, condemning the latter to a position of subservience. It would be an extraordinary grace if, from the ongoing synodical process, a new way of understanding pastoral ministry would spring forth, and paths would be set in motion so that the pastors of today and tomorrow could learn to better tune in to the "wavelengths" of the People of God, of which they themselves are members by virtue of baptism.

The third focus could be called *gradualness*. It is true, in fact, that the theme of synodality has made its appearance only gradually in the magisterium of Pope Francis. It still lacks an explicit thematization in the programmatic apostolic exhortation of the pontificate *Evangelii Gaudium*, where nevertheless all its presuppositions are outlined. It begins to surface occasionally in a few speeches, often in connection with the Assemblies of the Synod of Bishops, to find its first important fine tuning in 2015, on the occasion of the address for the fiftieth anniversary of the Synod. It continued thereafter to be enriched with further facets and, at the same time, to penetrate more and more into ecclesial sentiment. In this way, in a 2016 interview granted to *La Croix*, the Holy Father considered that the time was not ripe to celebrate a

Synod on synodality. Yet, three years later, at the end of the Special Assembly for the Amazon, the pope announced that synodality had received the most votes as the theme for the next Synod. And then, in 2020, he himself called for precisely the long-awaited Synod on synodality.

From then on, as is well known, an articulate process has begun in which we are still involved and of which we cannot foresee all the developments. The hope is that this publication may in its way prove to be a useful tool to accompany the ongoing journey, in which all of us—from the pope to the last of the baptized—are called to listen to the Holy Spirit, to hear what he "says to the Churches" (Rev. 2:7).

Cardinal Mario Grech
Secretary General of the Synod

Introduction

Sister Nathalie Becquart

Synodality According to Pope Francis: A Call from God, an Open Path, a Moving Thought

This book is a kind of compendium of Pope Francis's reflections on synodality. It contains all his main texts and statements on synodality since the beginning of his pontificate. These documents, of different styles, include letters or speeches addressed to all or, more specifically, to local churches (Germany, Chile . . .) or particular groups (bishops, theologians . . .) as well as excerpts from documents of the magisterium (encyclicals). It also includes speeches delivered during the various synods of bishops (Synod on the Family in 2014 and 2015, Synod on Youth in 2018, Synod on the Amazon in 2019, current Synod on Synodality) with excerpts of postsynodal exhortations (*Christus Vivit*, *Querida Amazonia*), homilies or words delivered during various meetings, general or private audiences, and interviews. All of this corpus allows us to delve into Pope Francis's rich thought on synodality, of which he has made a central plank of his pontificate, beginning with his election and his appearance on the balcony, with his way of relating immediately to the people there in St. Peter's Square. The choice to organize these texts in chronological order rather than by theme allows us to grasp how the harmonies of synodality unfold over time and circumstances through the events—particularly the Synods of Bishops—and the many meetings, audiences, and trips that dot the life of the Supreme Pontiff.

A careful reading of all these passages on synodality, which this book has the merit of bringing together, makes us perceive that Pope Francis's thought is a thought in motion that unfolds and deepens over time through successive synodal experiences. In the image of synodality, which is a dynamic vision of the church as the People of God on a journey through history, the pope's thought is an open thought, anchored in reality and experience, a dynamic thought that is never closed because it is a thought of discernment, an embodied thought that takes reality into account. The four basic principles that underlie the approach to synodality, as stated by Pope Francis in *Evangelii Gaudium*, are (1) "Time is greater than space"; (2) "Unity prevails over conflict"; (3) "Realites are more important than ideas"; (4) "The whole is greater than the part."[1]

The Pope of Synodality

The recurrence of the theme of synodality in the official speeches and writings of Pope Francis reflects the importance of this synodal dynamic for Pope Francis, who could be described as the pope of synodality, so much so that he highlights this constitutive dimension of the church by emphasizing its roots and implications for the concrete life of the church today. For him, synodality is first of all a call from God; it is the vocation of the church of the third millennium because it has been identified as the way to transmit the faith in today's world. This is how he makes it explicit in what can be considered one of the key texts of his pontificate, the Address for the 50th Anniversary of the Establishment of the Synod of Bishops of October 17, 2015: "The world in which we live, and which we are called to love and serve, even with its contradictions, demands that the Church strengthen cooperation in all areas of her mission. It is precisely this path of *synodality* which God expects of the Church of the third millennium." Synodality can thus be seen as an important key to his pontificate, which brings the church to a new stage in its reception of the Second Vatican Council. His conviction is that the church is fundamentally a people on the move, the People of God allowing themselves to be guided by the

[1]Pope Francis, Encyclical Letter *Evangelii Gaudium* (November 24, 2013), 217–37.

Holy Spirit, and so must pursue a path that leads to the "synodalization" of all ecclesial realities. In short, Pope Francis invites us to understand that it is not just a matter of *having a synod,* as we are currently experiencing it, but of *becoming a synod.* In the synodal church, which is a church of listening and dialogue, a relational and inclusive church of brothers and sisters in Christ, all the baptized are called to be protagonists, mission actors, missionary disciples to proclaim the Gospel in today's world—that is, to propose a personal encounter with Christ and to build human fraternity.

The Challenge of Putting Synodality into Practice

"Synodality is the dynamic dimension, the historical dimension of ecclesial communion founded on the Trinitarian communion, which by simultaneously appreciating the *sensus fidei* of the whole holy faithful people of God, apostolic collegiality, and unity with the Successor of Peter, must animate the conversion and reform of the Church at every level."[2] As well expressed in this quote, synodality—the realization of the church in history as communion in mission—is a journey of conversion, both personal and communal. We are in the process of relearning synodality, so the thought that arises and shapes synodality cannot but be a thought in motion, a sign of a Christian identity understood as a dynamic identity. It is, in a sense, a pilgrim thought that never ceases to be challenged and reinterrogated, a learning thought that progresses through the experience of synodality.

Thus, in a sense, these texts constitute a small manual of synodality, or rather a practical guide to synodality in action. We are not dealing here with a well-organized theological treatise, but rather with a collection of "road maps" that help us orient ourselves along the paths of synodality, which are not all mapped out

[2]Pope Francis, *Video Message on the Occasion of the Plenary of the Pontifical Commission for Latin America* (May 26, 2022).

in advance. Pope Francis's initial conviction, expressed in his first official speeches, is that "we must go down this road of synodality, growing in harmony with the service of primacy."[3] To do this "we must walk together: the people, the bishops and the Pope."[4] The church today is therefore relearning synodality, which is in fact an apprenticeship through experience. It is not enough to have the theoretical vision; the challenge is to put it into practice: "What the Lord is asking of us, in a sense, is already all contained in the word 'Synod.' Walking together—laity, pastors, Bishop of Rome—is an easy concept to put into words, but not so easy to put into practice."[5] As can be seen from the texts and speeches related to this institution, the Synods of Bishops under this pontificate have become true schools of synodality, concrete experiences of learning synodality through experience. Francis makes it the heart of his teaching on synodality by insisting on the spiritual attitudes necessary to live synodality: faith and trust in God, humility in listening and the courage to speak, prayer, dialogue and sharing, trust in others, and inner freedom.

The Key Elements Underlying Pope Francis's Synodal Vision

Through this path of synodality that Pope Francis offers us here, we can see the key elements that form the basis of his vision of the synodal church, received as a fruit of Vatican II and at the same time deeply rooted in the early church.

First, the image of the church as the people of God on a journey. Synodality is a "walking together" that invites us to see and

[3]Pope Francis, *Homily at the Holy Mass and Imposition of the Pallium to the New Metropolitans* (June 29, 2013).

[4]Pope Francis, *Interview with Father Antonio Spadaro, S.J.*, from *L'Osservatore Romano*, daily ed., Year CLIII, 216, Sat. 21/09/2013. See also "A Big Heart Open to God, an Interview with Pope Francis," *America*, September 30, 2013.

[5]Pope Francis, *Address for the 50th Anniversary of the Establishment of the Synod of Bishops* (October 17, 2015).

experience the church as a people of missionary pilgrims. Through synodality, the church "manifests and configures itself as the People of God on a journey and an assembly summoned by the risen Lord."[6] The current pontificate inaugurates a new reception of the Second Vatican Council by giving a central place to Chapter II of *Evangelii Gaudium*. Francis recalls that "to be Church is to be the People of God" (*EG*, 114). This is an opportunity to deepen what it means to be church. The notion of the People of God has led to understanding the church as a totality (*EG*, 17) living in "pluriform harmony" (*EG*, 220). All its members, or *christifideles*, women and men, are empowered by the Spirit to be subjects of right and action. One of the great fruits of this way of being church as the People of God is that it emphasizes the participation and coresponsibility of all equally; all the faithful are coresponsible in a differentiated way according to their gifts, ministries, and charisms.

The second key element is the theology of baptism as the foundation of missionary coresponsibility. Through baptism, all are priests, prophets, and kings. Synodality is a way to rediscover and put into practice the primacy of the baptismal vocation as a call to holiness and the common priesthood as a call to coresponsibility. The challenge is to promote dialogue and interaction among the People of God, especially between priests and laity.

Third, one must take into account the *sensus fidei* as described in *Lumen Gentium* 12, that is, the "sense of faith" of the whole People of God, what Pope Francis calls the faithful's "sense of smell."[7] This notion reflects the fact that it is to the church of God as a whole that the faith is revealed; she is its depository—hence, the challenge to listen to the *sensus fidei* that cannot "err in faith." This dimension, which was brought to light in the Second Vatican

---

[6]International Theological Commission, *Synodality in the Life and Mission of the Church* (March 2, 2018), 42.

[7]"The people have 'flair!' They have flair for finding new ways forward, they have the '*sensus fidei*,' theologians say. What could be better than that? And in the Synod there must also be what the Holy Spirit says to the laity, to the People of God, to everyone." Pope Francis, *Meeting with Clergy, Persons of Consecrated Life and Members of Pastoral Councils during His Pastoral Visit to Assisi* (October 4, 2013).

Council, underlies the synodal dynamic of discernment, which involves consultation with all the faithful. The sense of faith of all the faithful (i.e., the *sensus*) is as much a vital part of the church's teaching authority (i.e., the magisterium) as that of the hierarchy. Synodality is a means to recover the authority of the *sensus fidei* alongside the authority of the hierarchical magisterium and the magisterium of theologians. It is about living the primacy of the Successor of Peter and the collegiality of the bishops within the synodality of the entire People of God.

This brings us to the fourth key element—and perhaps the most central to understanding Pope Francis's vision of synodality—which is the action of the Holy Spirit. The synodal process is a spiritual process. A synodal church is a church listening to the Holy Spirit through hearing the Word of God and listening to one another. "The action of the Spirit in the communion of the Body of Christ and in the missionary journey of the People of God is the principle of synodality,"[8] and Pope Francis in his speeches keeps insisting that synodality is not a parliament but a process of discernment that presupposes a deep listening to the action of the Spirit in oneself and in the community. It is based on the act of faith that the Spirit works in all the baptized, regardless of their vocation, age, condition, or responsibility.

A fifth constitutive element of the synodal approach highlighted by Pope Francis is the recognition and consideration of the diversity of charisms. Synodality, the principle of the participation of all in the life of the church, reflects the fact that all the baptized are called to be active subjects, protagonists in the mission of the church, because the Holy Spirit confers different charisms on all members of the People of God, a charism being a particular gift received for the good of all. This synodal vision implies the recognition of the coessentiality of these two dimensions of the church, the hierarchical and the charismatic. On many occasions, Pope Francis stresses the importance of the participation of all and in particular

[8]International Theological Commission, *Synodality in the Life and Mission of the Church* (March 2, 2018), 46.

the role of young people and women, the place of consecrated life and movements, and the commitment of the various groups and organizations in the church that arise from this diversity of charisms. Thus, in *Christus Vivit,* this definition of youth ministry: "Youth ministry cannot but be synodal, that is, capable of shaping a 'walking together' that implies an appreciation of the charisms that the Spirit bestows according to the vocation and role of each of the members [of the Church], through a dynamism of co-responsibility. [. . .] Animated by this spirit, we will be able to move toward a Church that is participatory and co-responsible, capable of valuing the richness of the variety of which it is composed, also gratefully welcoming the contribution of the lay faithful, including young people and women, that of consecrated female and male life, and that of groups, associations and movements. No one should be put or be allowed to stand aside."[9]

Finally, the sixth and final element that can be identified through these texts as the foundation of this vision of synodality is the integration of a relational anthropology that underlies the conception of a relational church. Throughout his pontificate, Pope Francis has constantly called for building a "culture of encounter." In his manner of ministry, we see how much he places encounter at the center and unfolds the horizon of human fraternity as the axis of the church's mission. Indeed, *Laudato Si'* and *Fratelli Tutti,* which are, in a sense, GPSs for synodality, contain what is at the heart of synodality, a relational way of looking at the world and looking at the church: "everything is connected." Throughout these texts, delivered at various meetings, the call to synodality unfolds, which is the call to become more and more a relational church, living in fraternity and friendship in the Lord, a church of brothers and sisters in Christ, opening up to new communicative and relational dynamics in the church to serve the goal of living together in our common home. Thus, synodality makes us rediscover and reintegrate the primacy of the ecclesial "we" in the service of the

---

[9]Pope Francis, Apostolic Exhortation *Christus Vivit* (March 25, 2019), 206.

common good, our vocation to form an "us" because we belong to each other, we are interdependent. The relational anthropology on which synodal ecclesiology is based has reciprocity and circularity as key words.

Beyond the words and content developed in this book, it is interesting to see the diversity of groups and ecclesial actors Pope Francis addresses in these texts on synodality, which more often than not take the form of a conversation. One notices his attention to the diversity of local churches and the diversity of ecclesial actors with whom he shares his vision of synodality, but he does not fail to highlight the seeds of synodality that his interlocutors already carry within themselves. Ultimately, this "living magisterium" of Pope Francis on synodality at this stage of his pontificate, as presented here, invites us to pursue the path of synodality, that is, a creative and dynamic path, an open process, a "walking together" in the breath of the Holy Spirit and the breath of the Second Vatican Council–hence, the invitation to enter into the reading of this book as one enters into a pilgrimage with a large and generous heart, a heart that is humble and willing to receive the lights and graces that the Lord wants to bestow. Pope Francis invited us to experience the synod as "a time of grace"[10] and a journey of conversion. May the reading of these pages help us to enter into the spiritual experience of synodality that is an experience of the Trinitarian mystery and the mystery of the church.

[10]Pope Francis, *Moment of Reflection for the Beginning of the Synodal Path* (October 9, 2021).

In Harmony with the Primacy, United in Differences

Homily, Imposition of the Sacred Pallium on Metropolitan Archbishops

Vatican Basilica, June 29, 2013

To confirm in unity. Here I would like to reflect for a moment on the rite which we have carried out. The pallium is a symbol of communion with the Successor of Peter, "the lasting and visible source and foundation of the unity both of faith and of communion" (*Lumen Gentium*, 18). And your presence today, dear brothers, is the sign that the Church's communion does not mean uniformity. The Second Vatican Council, in speaking of the hierarchical structure of the Church, states that the Lord "established the apostles as college or permanent assembly, at the head of which he placed Peter, chosen from their number" (*ibid.*, 19). To confirm in unity: the Synod of Bishops, in harmony with the primate.

Let us go forward on the path of synodality, and grow in harmony with the service of the primacy. And the Council continues, "This college, in so far as it is composed of many members, is the expression of the variety and universality of the people of God" (*ibid.*, 22). In the Church, variety, which is itself a great treasure, is always grounded in the harmony of unity, like a great mosaic in which every small piece joins with others as part of God's one great plan. This should inspire us to work always to overcome every conflict which wounds the body of the Church. United in our differences: there is no other Catholic way to be united. This is the Catholic spirit, the Christian spirit: to be united in our differences. This is the way of Jesus! The pallium, while being a sign of communion with the Bishop of Rome and with the universal church, with the Synod of Bishops, also commits each of you to being a servant of communion.

The Continental Mission

Address to the Leadership of the Episcopal Conferences of Latin America

Rio de Janeiro, Brazil, July 28, 2013

I thank the Lord for this opportunity to speak with you, my brother bishops, the leadership of CELAM [El Consejo Episcopal Latinoamericano y Caribeño] for the four-year period from 2011 to 2015. For 57 years CELAM has served the 22 Episcopal Conferences of Latin America and the Caribbean, working in a spirit of solidarity and subsidiarity to promote, encourage and improve collegiality among the bishops and communion between the region's Churches and their pastors.

Like yourselves, I too witnessed the powerful working of the Spirit in the Fifth General Conference of the Latin American and Caribbean Episcopate in Aparecida, in May 2007, which continues to inspire the efforts of CELAM for the desired renewal of the Particular Churches. In many of them, this renewal is clearly taking place. I would like to focus this conversation on the legacy of that fraternal encounter, which all of us have chosen to call a Continental Mission. . . .

Dimensions of the Continental Mission

The Continental Mission is planned along two lines: the programmatic and the paradigmatic. The programmatic mission, as its name indicates, consists in a series of missionary activities. The paradigmatic mission, on the other hand, involves setting in a missionary key all the day-to-day activities of the Particular

Churches. Clearly this entails a whole process of reforming ecclesial structures. The "change of structures" (from obsolete ones to new ones) will not be the result of reviewing an organizational flow chart, which would lead to a static reorganization; rather it will result from the very dynamics of mission. What makes obsolete structures pass away, what leads to a change of heart in Christians, is precisely *missionary spirit*. Hence the importance of the paradigmatic mission.

The Continental Mission, both programmatic and paradigmatic, calls for creating a sense of a Church which is organized to serve all the baptized, and men and women of goodwill. Christ's followers are not individuals caught up in a privatized spirituality, but persons in community, devoting themselves to others. The Continental Mission thus implies *membership in the Church*.

An approach like this, which begins with missionary discipleship and involves understanding Christian identity as membership in the Church, demands that we clearly articulate *the real challenges* facing missionary discipleship. Here I will mention only two: the Church's inner renewal and dialogue with the world around us.

The Church's Inner Renewal

Aparecida considered Pastoral Conversion to be a necessity. This conversion involves believing in the Good News, believing in Jesus Christ as the bearer of God's Kingdom as it breaks into the world and in his victorious presence over evil, believing in the help and guidance of the Holy Spirit, believing in the Church, the Body of Christ and the prolonging of the dynamism of the incarnation.

Consequently, we, as pastors, need to ask questions about the actual state of the Churches which we lead. These questions can serve as a guide in examining where the dioceses stand in taking up the spirit of Aparecida; they are questions which we need to keep asking as an examination of conscience.

1. Do we see to it that our work, and that of our priests, is more pastoral than administrative? Who primarily benefits from

our efforts, the Church as an organization or the People of God as a whole?

2. Do we fight the temptation simply to react to complex problems as they arise? Are we creating a proactive mindset? Do we promote opportunities and possibilities to manifest God's mercy? Are we conscious of our responsibility for refocusing pastoral approaches and the functioning of Church structures for the benefit of the faithful and society?
3. In practice, do we make the lay faithful sharers in the Mission? Do we offer them the word of God and the sacraments with a clear awareness and conviction that the Holy Spirit makes himself manifest in them?
4. Is pastoral discernment a habitual criterion, through the use of Diocesan Councils? Do such Councils and Parish Councils, whether pastoral or financial, provide real opportunities for lay people to participate in pastoral consultation, organization and planning? The good functioning of these Councils is critical. I believe that on this score, we are far behind.
5. As pastors, bishops and priests, are we conscious and convinced of the mission of the lay faithful and do we give them the freedom to continue discerning, in a way befitting their growth as disciples, the mission which the Lord has entrusted to them? Do we support them and accompany them, overcoming the temptation to manipulate them or infantilize them? Are we constantly open to letting ourselves be challenged in our efforts to advance the good of the Church and her mission in the world?
6. Do pastoral agents and the faithful in general feel part of the Church, do they identify with her and bring her closer to the baptized who are distant and alienated?

As can be appreciated, what is at stake here are *attitudes*. Pastoral Conversion is chiefly concerned with attitudes and reforming our lives. A change of attitudes is necessarily something ongoing: "it is a process," and it can only be kept on track with the help of guidance and discernment. It is important always to keep in mind that the compass preventing us from going astray is that of Catholic identity, understood as membership in the Church.

Dialogue with the World around Us

We do well to recall the words of the Second Vatican Council: "The joys and hopes, the grief and anguish of the people of our time, especially of those who are poor or afflicted, are the joys and hopes, the grief and anguish of the followers of Christ as well" (*Gaudium et Spes*, 1). Here we find the basis for our dialogue with the contemporary world.

Responding to the existential issues of people today, especially the young, listening to the language they speak, can lead to a fruitful change, which must take place with the help of the Gospel, the magisterium, and the Church's social doctrine. The scenarios and the areopagi involved are quite varied. For example, a single city can contain various collective imaginations which create "different cities." If we remain within the parameters of our "traditional culture," which was essentially rural, we will end up nullifying the power of the Holy Spirit. God is everywhere: we have to know how to find him in order to be able to proclaim him in the language of each and every culture; every reality, every language, has its own rhythm.

Some Temptations against Missionary Discipleship

The decision for missionary discipleship will encounter temptation. It is important to know where the evil spirit is afoot in order to aid our discernment. It is not a matter of chasing after demons, but simply one of clear-sightedness and evangelical astuteness. I will mention only a few attitudes which are evidence of a Church which is "tempted." It has to do with recognizing certain contemporary proposals which can parody the process of missionary discipleship and hold back, even bring to a halt, the process of Pastoral Conversion.

1. *Making the Gospel message an ideology*. This is a temptation which has been present in the Church from the beginning: the attempt to interpret the Gospel apart from the Gospel itself and apart from the Church. An example: Aparecida, at one particular moment, felt this temptation. It employed, and rightly so, the method of "see, judge and act" (cf. No. 19). The temptation, though, was to opt for a way of "seeing" which was completely "antiseptic," detached and unengaged, which is impossible. The way we "see" is always affected by the way we direct our gaze. There is no such thing as an "antiseptic" hermeneutics. The question was, rather: How are we going to look at reality in order to see it? Aparecida replied: With the eyes of discipleship. This is the way Nos. 20–32 are to be understood. There are other ways of making the message an ideology, and at present proposals of this sort are appearing in Latin America and the Caribbean. I mention only a few:
    a. Sociological reductionism. This is the most readily available means of making the message an ideology. At certain times it has proved extremely influential. It involves an interpretative claim based on a hermeneutics drawn from the social sciences. It extends to the most varied fields, from market liberalism to Marxist categorization.
    b. Psychologizing. Here we have to do with an elitist hermeneutics which ultimately reduces the "encounter with Jesus Christ" and its development to a process of growing self-awareness. It is ordinarily to be found in spirituality courses, spiritual retreats, etc. It ends up being an immanent, self-centered approach. It has nothing to do with transcendence and consequently, with missionary spirit.
    c. The Gnostic solution. Closely linked to the previous temptation, it is ordinarily found in elite groups offering a higher spirituality, generally disembodied, which ends up in a preoccupation with certain pastoral "*quaestiones disputatae.*" It was the first deviation

in the early community and it reappears throughout the Church's history in ever new and revised versions. Generally its adherents are known as "enlightened Catholics" (since they are in fact rooted in the culture of the Enlightenment).

d. The Pelagian solution. This basically appears as a form of restorationism. In dealing with the Church's problems, a purely disciplinary solution is sought, through the restoration of outdated manners and forms which, even on the cultural level, are no longer meaningful. In Latin America it is usually to be found in small groups, in some new religious congregations, in exaggerated tendencies toward doctrinal or disciplinary "safety." Basically it is static, although it is capable of inversion, in a process of regression. It seeks to "recover" the lost past.

1. *Functionalism.* Its effect on the Church is paralyzing. More than being interested in the road itself, it is concerned with fixing holes in the road. A functionalist approach has no room for mystery; it aims at efficiency. It reduces the reality of the Church to the structure of an NGO. What counts are quantifiable results and statistics. The Church ends up being run like any other business organization. It applies a sort of "theology of prosperity" to the organization of pastoral work.
2. *Clericalism* is also a temptation very present in Latin America. Curiously, in the majority of cases, it has to do with a sinful complicity: the priest clericalizes the lay person and the lay person kindly asks to be clericalized, because deep down it is easier. The phenomenon of clericalism explains, in great part, the lack of maturity and Christian freedom in some of the Latin American laity. Either they simply do not grow (the majority), or else they take refuge in forms of ideology like those we have just seen, or in partial and limited ways of belonging. Yet in our countries there does exist a form of freedom of the laity which finds expression in communal experiences: Catholic as community. Here one sees a greater

autonomy, which on the whole is a healthy thing, basically expressed through popular piety. The chapter of the Aparecida document on popular piety describes this dimension in detail. The spread of Bible study groups, of ecclesial basic communities and of Pastoral Councils is in fact helping to overcome clericalism and to increase lay responsibility.

We could continue by describing other temptations against missionary discipleship, but I consider these to be the most important and influential at present for Latin America and the Caribbean.

Some Ecclesiological Guidelines

1. The missionary discipleship which Aparecida proposed to the Churches of Latin America and the Caribbean is the journey which God desires for the present "today." Every utopian (future-oriented) or restorationist (past-oriented) impulse is spiritually unhealthy. God is real and he shows himself in the "today." With regard to the past, his presence is given to us as "memory" of his saving work, both in his people and in each of us as individuals; with regard to the future, he gives himself to us as "promise" and hope. In the past God was present and left his mark: memory helps us to encounter him; in the future is promise alone . . . he is not in the thousand and one "futuribles." The "today" is closest to eternity; even more: the "today" is a flash of eternity. In the "today," eternal life is in play.

Missionary discipleship is a vocation: a call and an invitation. It is given in the "today," but also "in tension." There is no such thing as static missionary discipleship. A missionary disciple cannot be his own master, his immanence is in tension towards the transcendence of discipleship and towards the transcendence of mission. It does not allow for self-absorption: either it points to Jesus Christ or it points to the people to whom he must be proclaimed. The missionary disciple is a self-transcending subject, a subject projected towards encounter: an encounter with the Master (who anoints us as his disciples) and an encounter with men and women who await the message.

That is why I like saying that the position of missionary disciples is not in the center but at the periphery: they live poised towards the peripheries . . . including the peripheries of eternity, in the encounter with Jesus Christ. In the preaching of the Gospel, to speak of "existential peripheries" decentralizes things; as a rule, we are afraid to leave the center. The missionary disciple is someone "off center": the center is Jesus Christ, who calls us and sends us forth. The disciple is sent to the existential peripheries.

2. The Church is an institution, but when she makes herself a "center," she becomes merely functional, and slowly but surely turns into a kind of NGO. The Church then claims to have a light of her own, and she stops being that *mysterium lunae* of which the Church Fathers spoke. She becomes increasingly self-referential and loses her need to be missionary. From an "institution" she becomes an "enterprise." She stops being a bride and ends up being an administrator; from being a servant, she becomes an "inspector." Aparecida wanted a Church which is bride, mother, and servant, more a facilitator of faith than an inspector of faith.
3. In Aparecida, two pastoral categories stand out; they arise from the uniqueness of the Gospel, and we can employ them as guidelines for assessing how we are living missionary discipleship in the Church: *nearness and encounter*. Neither of these two categories is new; rather, they are the way God has revealed himself to us in history. He is the "God who is near" to his people, a nearness which culminates in the incarnation. He is the God who goes forth to meet his people. In Latin America and the Caribbean there are pastoral plans which are "distant," disciplinary pastoral plans which give priority to principles, forms of conduct, organizational procedures . . . and clearly lack nearness, tenderness, a warm touch. They do

not take into account the "revolution of tenderness" brought by the incarnation of the Word. There are pastoral plans designed with such a dose of distance that they are incapable of sparking an encounter: an encounter with Jesus Christ, an encounter with our brothers and sisters. Such pastoral plans can at best provide a dimension of proselytism, but they can never inspire people to feel part of or belong to the Church. Nearness creates communion and belonging; it makes room for encounter. Nearness takes the form of dialogue and creates a culture of encounter. One touchstone for measuring whether a pastoral plan embodies nearness and a capacity for encounter is the homily. What are our homilies like? Do we imitate the example of our Lord, who spoke "as one with authority," or are they simply moralizing, detached, abstract?

4. Those who direct pastoral work, the Continental Mission (both programmatic and paradigmatic), are the bishops. Bishops must lead, which is not the same thing as being authoritarian. As well as pointing to the great figures of the Latin American episcopate, which we all know, I would like to add a few things about the profile of the bishop, which I already presented to the Nuncios at our meeting in Rome. Bishops must be pastors, close to people, fathers and brothers, and gentle, patient and merciful. Men who love poverty, both interior poverty, as freedom before the Lord, and exterior poverty, as simplicity and austerity of life. Men who do not think and behave like "princes." Men who are not ambitious, who are married to one church without having their eyes on another. Men capable of watching over the flock entrusted to them and protecting everything that keeps it together: guarding their people out of concern for the dangers which could threaten them, but above all instilling hope: so that light will shine in people's hearts. Men capable of supporting with love and patience God's dealings with his people. The Bishop has to be among his people in three ways: in front of them, pointing the way; among them, keeping them together and preventing them from being scattered; and behind them,

> ensuring that no one is left behind, but also, and primarily, so that the flock itself can sniff out new paths.

I do not wish to go into further detail about the person of the Bishop, but simply to add, including myself in this statement, that we are lagging somewhat as far as Pastoral Conversion is concerned. We need to help one another a bit more in taking the steps that the Lord asks of us in the "today" of Latin America and the Caribbean. And this is a good place to start.

I thank you for your patience in listening to me. Pardon me if my remarks have been somewhat disjointed and please, I beg that we take seriously our calling as servants of the holy and faithful people of God, for this is where authority is exercised and demonstrated: in the ability to serve. Many thanks.

Walk Together

Interview with Pope Francis
by Fr. Antonio Spadaro

L'Osservatore Romano, September 2013

On June 29, during the ceremony of the blessing and imposition of the pallium on 34 metropolitan archbishops, Pope Francis spoke about "the path of collegiality" as the road that can lead the church to "grow in harmony with the service of primacy." So I ask: "How can we reconcile in harmony Petrine primacy and collegiality? Which roads are feasible also from an ecumenical perspective?"

The pope responds, "We must walk together: the people, the bishops and the pope. Synodality should be lived at various levels. Maybe it is time to change the methods of the Synod of Bishops, because it seems to me that the current method is not dynamic. This will also have ecumenical value, especially with our Orthodox brethren. From them we can learn more about the meaning of episcopal collegiality and the tradition of synodality. The joint effort of reflection, looking at how the church was governed in the early centuries, before the breakup between East and West, will bear fruit in due time. In ecumenical relations it is important not only to know each other better, but also to recognize what the Spirit has sown in the other as a gift for us. I want to continue the discussion that was begun in 2007 by the joint [Catholic–Orthodox] commission on how to exercise the Petrine primacy, which led to the signing of the Ravenna Document. We must continue on this path."

I ask how Pope Francis envisions the future unity of the church in light of this response. He answers: "We must walk united with our differences: there is no other way to become one. This is the way of Jesus."

The Bishop, Guardian of the Gift of Harmony in Diversity

Meeting with the Clergy, Consecrated People, and Members of Diocesan Pastoral Councils

CATHEDRAL OF SAN RUFINO, ASSISI, OCTOBER 4, 2013

Dear Brothers and Sisters of the Diocesan Community, Good Afternoon!

Thank you for your welcome, priests, men and women religious, laity engaged in pastoral councils! How needed pastoral councils are! A bishop cannot guide a diocese without pastoral councils. A parish priest cannot guide the parish without the parish council. This is fundamental! We are in the Cathedral! Here is the baptismal font where Sts. Francis and Clare were baptized; in their day it was located in the Church of Santa Maria. The memory of one's Baptism is important! Baptism is our birth as children of Holy Mother Church. I would like to ask you a question: who among you knows the day you were baptized? So few, so few . . . now, here is your homework! Mother, Father, tell me: when was I baptized? It's very important, because it was the day of your birth as a child of God. One Spirit, one Baptism, in a variety of charisms and ministries. What a great gift it is to be the Church, to be a part of the People of God! Together we are the People of God. In harmony, in the communion of gift of harmony in diversity which is the work of the Holy Spirit, because the Holy Spirit is harmony and creates harmony: it is his gift, and we should be open to receive it.

The Bishop is the guardian of this harmony. The bishop is the guardian of this diversity. That is why Pope Benedict wished that the pastoral activity in the Franciscan papal basilicas be integrated into the diocesan one. For he has to create harmony: it is his task, his duty and his vocation. I am glad that you are advancing nicely on this road, and to the benefit of all, by peacefully working together. I encourage you to continue in this. The pastoral visit that has just ended and the diocesan synod which you are about to celebrate are intense moments of growth for this Church which God has blessed in a special way. The Church grows, but not through proselytizing: no, no! The Church does not grow through proselytizing. The Church grows through attraction, through the attraction of the witness that each one of us gives to the People of God.

Now, briefly, I would like to highlight several aspects of your life as a Community. I do not wish to tell you something new, but rather to confirm you in those things which are most important, and which mark your journey as a diocese.

1. The first thing is *to listen to God's Word.* This is what the Church is: as the Bishop said, it is the community that listens with faith and love to the Lord who speaks. The pastoral plan that you are living out together insists precisely on this fundamental dimension. It is the Word of God that inspires faith, which nourishes and revitalizes it. And it is the Word of God that touches hearts, converts them to God and to his logic which is so different from our own. It is the Word of God that continually renews our communities . . .

I think we can all improve a bit in this respect: by becoming better listeners of the Word of God, in order to be less rich on our own words and richer in his words. I think of the priest who has the task of preaching. How can he preach if he has not first opened his heart, not listened in silence to the Word of God? Away with these never ending, boring homilies that no one understands. This is for you! I think of fathers and mothers, who are the primary educators [of their children]: how can they educate them if their consciences have not been enlightened by the Word of God. If their way of thinking and acting is not guided by the Word, what sort of example can they possibly give to their children? This is important, because then mothers and fathers complain: "Oh, this child. . . ." But you, what witness have you given the child? How have you spoken to him? Have you talked with him about the Word of God or about TV news? Fathers and mothers need to be talking about the Word of God! And I think of catechists and of all those who are involved in education: if their hearts have not been warmed by the Word, how can they warm the hearts of others, of children, of youth, of adults? It is not enough just to read the Sacred Scriptures, we need to listen to Jesus who speaks in them: it is Jesus himself who speaks in the Scriptures, it is Jesus who speaks in them. We need to be receiving antennas that are tuned in to the Word of God, in order to become broadcasting antennas! One receives and transmits. It is the Spirit of God who makes the Scriptures come alive, who makes us understand them deeply and in accord with their authentic and full meaning! Let us ask ourselves as the Synod draws near: what place does the Word of God have in my life, in my everyday life? Am I tuned in to God or in to the many buzz words or in to myself? This is a question that every one of us needs to ask him- or herself.

2. The second aspect is *walking*. It is one of my favorite words when I think about a Christian and about the Church. However, it has a special meaning for you: you are about to enter into the diocesan Synod. To hold a "synod" means to walk together. I think this is truly the most wonderful experience we can have: to belong to a people walking, journeying through history together with their Lord who walks among us! We are not alone, we do not walk alone. We are part of the one flock of Christ that walks together.

Here I think once more of you priests, and let me place myself in your company. What could be more beautiful for us than walking with our people? It is beautiful! When I think of the parish priests who knew the names of their parishioners, who went to visit them; even as one of them told me: "I know the name of each family's dog." They even knew the dog's name! How nice it was! What could be more beautiful than this? I repeat it often: walking with our people, sometimes in front, sometimes behind and sometimes in the middle, and sometimes behind: in front in order to guide the community, in the middle in order to encourage and support; and at the back in order to keep it united and so that no one lags too, too far behind, to keep them united. There is another reason too: because the people have a "nose"! The people scent out, discover, new ways to walk, they have the "*sensus fidei*," as theologians call it. What could be more beautiful than this? During the Synod, it will be very important to consider what the Holy Spirit is saying to the laity, to the People of God, to everyone.

But the most important thing is to walk together by working together, by helping one another, by asking forgiveness, by acknowledging one's mistakes and asking for forgiveness, and also by accepting the apologies of others by forgiving—how important this is! Sometimes I think of married people who separate after many years. "Oh . . . no, we didn't understand each other, we drifted apart." Perhaps at times they didn't know how to ask for forgiveness at the right time. Perhaps at times they did not know how to forgive. And I always give this advice to newlyweds: "Argue as much as you like. If the plates fly, let them! But never end the day without making peace! Never!" And if married people learn to say, "Excuse me, I was tired," or even a little gesture, this is peace. Then carry on with life the next day. This is a beautiful secret, and it prevents these painful separations. It is important to walk in unity, without running ahead, without nostalgia for the past. And while you walk you talk, you get to know one another, you tell one other about yourself, you grow as a family. Here let us ask ourselves: how do we walk? How does our diocese walk? Does it walk together? And what am I doing so that it may truly walk in unity? I do not wish to enter into a discussion here about gossip, but you know that gossip always divides.

3. Therefore: to listen, to walk, and the third aspect is missionary: *to proclaim even to the outskirts*. I also borrowed this from you, from your pastoral plan. The Bishop spoke recently about it. However, I wish to emphasize it, because it is something I also

experienced a great deal when I was in Buenos Aires: the importance of going out to meet the other in the outskirts, which are places, but which are primarily people living in particular situations in life. This was true in my former diocese, that of Buenos Aires. The outskirt which hurt me a great deal was to find children in middle-class families who didn't know how to make the Sign of the Cross. But you see, this is an outskirt! And I ask you, here in this diocese, are there children who do not know how to make the Sign of the Cross? Think about it. These are true outskirts of existence where God is absent.

In one sense, the outskirts of this diocese, for example, are the areas of the diocese that risk being left on the margins, beyond the street lights. But they are also people and human realities that are marginalized and despised. They are people who perhaps live physically close to the "center" but who spiritually are very far away.

Do not be afraid to go out and meet these people and situations. Do not allow yourselves to be impeded by prejudice, by habit, by an intellectual or pastoral rigidity, by the famous "we've always done it this way!" However, we can only go to the outskirts if we carry the Word of God in our hearts and if we walk with the Church, like St Francis. Otherwise, we take ourselves, not the Word of God, and this isn't good, it doesn't help anyone! We are not the ones who save the world: it is the Lord himself who saves it!

There you are, dear friends. I haven't given you any new recipes. I don't have any, and don't believe anyone who says he does: they don't exist. However, I did find several beautiful and important aspects of the journey of your Church that should be developed, and I want to confirm you in these. Listen to the Word, walk together as brothers and sisters, proclaim the Gospel to the outskirts! May the Lord bless you, may Our Lady protect you, and may St Francis help you all to experience the joy of being disciples of the Lord! Thank you.

Exchange of Gifts for Truth and Goodness

Apostolic Exhortation Evangelii Gaudium (no. 246)

NOVEMBER 24, 2013

How many important things unite us! If we really believe in the abundantly free working of the Holy Spirit, we can learn so much from one another! It is not just about being better informed about others, but rather about reaping what the Spirit has sown in them, which is also meant to be a gift for us. To give but one example, in the dialogue with our Orthodox brothers and sisters, we Catholics have the opportunity to learn more about the meaning of episcopal collegiality and their experience of synodality. Through an exchange of gifts, the Spirit can lead us ever more fully into truth and goodness.

An Institution That Puts Peter in Dialogue with His Brethren

Letter to Cardinal Lorenzo Baldisseri, Secretary General of the Synod of Bishops

April 1, 2014

Your Eminence,

On 15 September 1965 my Venerable Predecessor, the Servant of God, Paul VI—after having attentively examined the signs of the times, and aware of the need to strengthen by closer bonds the union of the Bishop of Rome with the Bishops whom the *Holy Spirit had constituted to govern the Church of God*—established the *Synod of Bishops* with the *Motu Proprio "Apostolica Sollicitudo."*

At that time, as the Second Vatican Council drew to a close, the emerging Synodal Body spurred all Catholic Bishops to share in the Bishop of Rome's concern for the Universal Church in a clearer and more effective way.

The Synodal Assemblies, which from that time have been celebrated in the presence of Bishops from the various continents, have made known the Church's activity concerning essential contributions to the problems in the world and they have offered the Successor of Peter valuable help and guidance in order to safeguard and increase the faith, in order to courageously offer the integrity of Christian life and strengthen the discipline of the Church.

In underlining the efficacy of the Synod and in recognizing the enormous good that they do for the Church, Blessed John Paul II, who presided over many Synodal Assemblies, suggested with foresight that: "*Perhaps this instrument could also be improved. Perhaps collegial pastoral responsibility could be expressed in the Synod even more fully*" (*Address at the Conclusion of the 6th General Assembly of the Synod of Bishops*, October 29, 1983). Indeed the breadth and depth of the objective given to the Synodal institution originated in the inexhaustible expanse of the mystery and of the horizon of the Church of God, namely communion and mission. Thus we can and must search for ever deeper and more authentic forms in exercising synodal collegiality to better realize ecclesial communion and to promote her inexhaustible mission.

Almost 50 years have passed since the Synod of Bishops was established, and I too having deeply examined the signs of the times and with the awareness that in the exercise of my Petrine Ministry it is necessary more than ever to further revitalize the close relationship between all the Pastors of the Church, I wish to value this precious heritage of the Council.

In this regard, there is no doubt that the Bishop of Rome is in need of the presence of his Brother Bishops, of their guidance and of their prudence and experience. Indeed, the Successor of Peter must proclaim to all "*Christ, the Son of the Living God*," and at the same time he must pay attention to what the Holy Spirit inspires on the lips of those who—accept the word of Jesus, who declares: "*You are Peter*" (cf. Mt 16:16–18)—fully participate in the Apostolic College.

I am, therefore, very grateful to those, who through their generous, diligent and competent work, have assured during all these years that the synodal institution contribute to the essential dialogue between Peter and his brothers. I would like to express my special recognition to Your Eminence, to the Members of the various Councils, to the Superiors and to the Officials of the Secretariat General, those present and past.

Now, in order to make more visible the much appreciated service that this Organism performs to promote the episcopal collegiality with the Bishop of Rome, I have decided to raise the Undersecretary to the dignity of bishop.

In this way, the Undersecretary, whose mandate already foresees cooperating with Your Eminence in developing the synodal activity, in virtue of the Episcopal Order, will mirror that affective and effective communion which constitutes the Synod of Bishops' primary purpose. In coordinating also the internal work of the General Secretariat, the Undersecretary will be called upon to voice the fertile and fruitful reality that flows from the participation in the episcopal munus, a source of sanctification for those who surround him, and foundation of hierarchical communion with the Bishop of Rome, head of the Episcopal College, and the Members of the said College.

I inform you of this, Your Eminence, with my Apostolic Blessing.

Gift of Listening and Openness to Discussion

Address during the Meeting on the Family

Saint Peter's Square, October 4, 2014

Dear Families, Good Evening!

Evening falls on our assembly. It is the hour at which one willingly returns home to meet at the same table, in the depth of affection, of the good that has been done and received, of the encounters which warm the heart and make it grow, good wine which hastens the unending feast in the days of man.

It is also the weightiest hour for one who finds himself face to face with his own loneliness, in the bitter twilight of shattered dreams and broken plans; how many people trudge through the day in the blind alley of resignation, of abandonment, even resentment: in how many homes the wine of joy has been less plentiful, and therefore, also the zest—the very wisdom—for life. Let us make our prayer heard for one another this evening, a prayer for all.

It is significant how—even in the individualistic culture which distorts bonds and renders them ephemeral—in each person born of woman, there remains alive an essential need for stability, for an open door, for someone with whom to weave and to share the story of life, a history to belong to. The communion of life embraced by spouses, their openness to the gift of life, the mutual protection, the encounter and the memory of generations, educational support, the transmission of the Christian faith to their children. . . . With all this, the family continues to be a school unparalleled in humanity, an indispensable contribution to a just and supportive society (cf. Apostolic Exhortation *Evangelii Gaudium*, nn. 66–68). And the deeper its roots, the more possible it is in life to go out and go far, without getting lost or feeling a stranger in a foreign land. This horizon helps us to grasp the importance of the Synod Assembly which opens tomorrow.

The *convenire in unum* around the Bishop of Rome is indeed an event of grace, in which episcopal collegiality is made manifest in a path of spiritual and pastoral discernment. To find what the Lord asks of his Church today, we must lend an ear to the debates of our time and perceive the "fragrance" of the men of this age, so as to be permeated with their joys and hopes, with their griefs and anxieties (cf. *Gaudium et Spes*, n. 1). At that moment we will know how to propose the good news on the family with credibility.

We know, in fact, that in the Gospel, there is a strength and tenderness capable of defeating that which creates unhappiness and violence. Yes, in the Gospel there is salvation which fulfills the most profound needs of man! Of this salvation—the work of God's mercy and grace—as a Church, we are a sign and instrument, a living and effective sacrament (cf. Apostolic Exhortation *Evangelii Gaudium*, n. 112). Were it not so, our edifice would be only a house of cards, and pastors would be reduced to clerics of state, on whose lips the people would search in vain for the freshness and "the fragrance of the Gospel" (*ibid.*, 39).

The essence of our prayer thus emerges within this framework. For the Synod Fathers we ask the Holy Spirit first of all for the gift of *listening*: to listen to God, that with him we may hear the cry of the people; to listen to the people until breathing in the will to which God calls us.

Along with listening, we invoke openness toward a sincere, open and fraternal *discussion*, which leads us to carry with pastoral responsibility the questions that this epochal change brings with it. Let us allow it to flow back into our hearts, never losing peace, but with serene trust which in his own time the Lord will not fail to lead us back into unity. Does Church history not perhaps—we know it does—recount many similar situations, which our Fathers were able to overcome with persistent patience and creativity?

The secret lies in a *gaze*: and it is the third gift that we implore with our prayer. Because, if we truly intend to walk among contemporary challenges, the decisive condition is to maintain a fixed gaze on Jesus Christ, to pause in contemplation and in adoration of his Face. If we accept his way of thinking, of living and of relating, we will never tire of translating the Synod work into guidelines and paths for the pastoral care of the person and of the family. Indeed, every time we return to the source of the Christian experience, new paths and undreamed-of possibilities open up. This can be intuited from the Gospel: "Do whatever he tells you" (Jn 2:5). These are words which contain the spiritual testament of Mary, "the friend who is ever concerned that wine not be lacking in our lives" (Apostolic Exhortation *Evangelii Gaudium*, n. 286). Let us make these words our own!

At that point, the three things: our *listening* and our *discussion* on the family, loved with the *gaze* of Christ, will become a providential occasion with which to renew—according to the example of St Francis—the Church and society. With the joy of the Gospel we will rediscover the way of a reconciled and merciful Church, poor and a friend of the poor; a Church "given strength that it might, in patience and in love, overcome its sorrows and its challenges, both within itself and from without" (*Lumen Gentium*, n. 8).

May the Wind of Pentecost blow upon the work of the Synod, on the Church, and on the whole of humanity. May it untie the knots which prevent people from encountering one another, heal the wounds that bleed, and rekindle much hope; there are so many people without hope! May we be granted this creative charity which allows one to love as Jesus loved. And may our message reclaim the vivacity and enthusiasm of the first missionaries of the Gospel.

Speak with Boldness, Listen with Humility

Greeting to the Synod Fathers during the First General Congregation of the Third Extraordinary General Assembly of the Synod of Bishops

October 6, 2014

Your Eminences, Your Beatitudes, Your Excellencies, Brothers and Sisters,

I give you my warm welcome to this meeting and I thank you from my heart for your caring and qualified presence and assistance. . . .

You bring the voice of the Particular Churches, assembled at the level of local Churches through the Bishops' Conferences. The Universal Church and the Particular Churches are divine institutions; the local Churches are thus understood as human institutions. You will give voice in *synodality*. It is a great responsibility: to bring the realities and problems of the Churches, in order to help them to walk on that path that is the Gospel of the family.

One general and basic condition is this: speaking honestly. Let no one say: "I cannot say this, they will think this or this of me. . . ." It is necessary to say with *parrhesia* [ed., "frankness, boldness of speech"] all that one feels. After the last Consistory (February 2014), in which the family was discussed, a Cardinal wrote to me, saying: what a shame that several Cardinals did not have the courage to say certain things out of respect for the Pope, perhaps believing that the Pope might think something else. This is not good, this is not *synodality*, because it is necessary to say all that, in the Lord, one feels the need to say: without polite deference, without hesitation. And, at the same time, one must listen with humility and welcome, with an open heart, what your brothers say. *Synodality* is exercised with these two approaches.

For this reason I ask of you, please, to employ these approaches as brothers in the Lord: speaking with *parrhesia* and listening with humility.

And do so with great tranquility and peace, so that the Synod may always unfold *cum Petro et sub Petro*, and the presence of the Pope is a guarantee for all and a safeguard of the faith.

Dear brothers, let us all collaborate so that the dynamic of *synodality* shines forth.

Thank you.

Synod Methods

Introductory Remarks, Synod for the Family

VATICAN, OCTOBER 5, 2015

Dear Beatitudes, Eminences, Excellencies, Brothers and Sisters,

We know, the Synod is a journey undertaken together in the spirit of *collegiality* and *synodality*, on which participants bravely adopt *parrhesia*, pastoral zeal and doctrinal wisdom, frankness, always keeping before our eyes the good of the Church, of families and the *suprema lex*, the *Salus animarum* (cf. can. 1752).

I should mention that the Synod is neither a convention nor a "parlor," neither a parliament nor a senate, where people make deals and reach a consensus. The Synod is rather an *ecclesial expression*, i.e., the Church that journeys together to understand reality with the eyes of faith and with the heart of God; it is the Church that questions herself with regard to her fidelity to the *deposit of faith*, which does not represent for the Church a museum to view, nor just something to safeguard, but is a living spring from which the Church drinks, to satisfy the thirst of, and illuminate the *deposit of life*.

The Synod works necessarily within the bosom of the Church and of the Holy People of God, to which we belong in the quality of shepherds—which is to say, as servants.

The Synod is also a protected space in which the Church experiences the action of the Holy Spirit. In the Synod, the Spirit speaks by means of the tongue of every person, who lets himself be guided by God, who always surprises, God, who reveals himself to little ones, who hides from the wise and intelligent; God who created the law and the Sabbath for man and not *vice versa*; by God, who leaves the 99 sheep to go in search of the one lost sheep; God who is always greater than our logic and our calculations.

Let us remember, however, that the Synod will be a space for the action of the Holy Spirit only if we participants put on *apostolic courage, evangelical humility* and *trusting prayer*.

Assume *apostolic courage* which refuses to be intimidated in the face of the temptations of the world that tend to extinguish the light of truth in the hearts of men, replacing it with small and temporary lights; nor even before the petrification of some hearts, which, despite good intentions, drive people away from God. The "apostolic courage to live life and not to make a museum of memories of our Christian life" (*Homily at Santa Marta*, April 28, 2015).

Assume *evangelical humility* that is able to overcome its own conventions and prejudices in order to listen to Brother Bishops and be filled with God. Humility that leads neither to pointing a finger at, nor to judging others, but to hands outstretched helping people to rise again without ever feeling superior.

Practice *trusting prayer* that is the action of the heart when it opens to God, when our humors are silenced in order to listen to the gentle voice of God, which speaks in silence. Without listening to God, all our "*words*" are only words that meet no need and serve no end. Without allowing ourselves to be guided by the Spirit, all our decisions will be but "*decorations*" that, instead of exalting the Gospel, cover and hide it.

Dear brothers, as I have said, the Synod is not a parliament in which to reach a consensus or a common accord by taking recourse to negotiation, to deal-making, or to compromise: indeed, the only method of the Synod is to open oneself up to the Holy Spirit with apostolic courage, with evangelical humility and confident, trusting prayer, in order that he guide us, enlighten us and make us keep before our eyes, not our personal opinions, but with faith in God, fidelity to the Magisterium, the good of the Church and the *salus animarum*. . . .

We begin our journey by invoking the help of the Holy Spirit and the intercession of the Holy Family: Jesus, Mary and St. Joseph! Thank you.

The Synod: A Convergence of a Listening Dynamism and Fellowship

Address on the 50th Anniversary of the Institution of the Synod of Bishops

OCTOBER 17, 2015

Your Beatitudes, Your Eminences, Your Excellencies,
Brothers and Sisters,

As the Ordinary General Assembly is in full session, this commemoration of the fiftieth anniversary of the institution of the Synod of Bishops is, for all of us, a cause for joy, praise and thanksgiving to the Lord. From the time of the Second Vatican Council until the present Assembly, we have experienced ever more intensely the necessity and beauty of "journeying together." . . .

From the beginning of my ministry as Bishop of Rome, I sought to enhance the Synod, which is one of the most precious legacies of the Second Vatican Council.[1] For Blessed Paul VI, the Synod of Bishops was meant to reproduce the image of the Ecumenical Council and reflect its spirit and method.[2] Pope Paul foresaw that the organization of the Synod could "be improved upon with the passing of time."[3] Twenty years later, Saint John Paul II echoed that thought when he stated that "this instrument might be further improved. Perhaps collegial pastoral responsibility could be more fully

[1]Cf. Francis, *Letter to the General Secretary of the Synod of Bishops, Cardinal Lorenzo Baldisseri, on the elevation of the Undersecretary, Msgr Fabio Fabene, to the episcopal dignity*, 1 April 2014.

[2]Cf. Blessed Paul VI, *Address for the Opening of the first Ordinary General Assembly of the Synod of Bishops*, 30 September 1967

[3]Blessed Paul VI, Motu proprio *Apostolica Sollicitudo* (15 September 1965), Proemium.

expressed in the Synod."[4] In 2006, Benedict XVI approved several changes to the *Ordo Synodi Episcoporum*, especially in light of the provisions of the *Code of Canon Law* and the *Code of Canons of the Eastern Churches*, which had been promulgated in the meantime.[5]

We must continue along this path. The world in which we live, and which we are called to love and serve, even with its contradictions, demands that the Church strengthen cooperation in all areas of her mission. It is precisely this path of *synodality* which God expects of the Church of the third millennium.

* * *

What the Lord is asking of us is already in some sense present in the very word "synod." Journeying together—laity, pastors, the Bishop of Rome—is an easy concept to put into words, but not so easy to put into practice.

After stating that the people of God comprise all the baptized who are called to "be a spiritual house and a holy priesthood,"[6] the Second Vatican Council went on to say that "the whole body of the faithful, who have an anointing which comes from the holy one (cf. 1 *Jn* 2:20, 27), cannot err in matters of belief. This characteristic is shown in the supernatural sense of the faith (*sensus fidei*) of the whole people of God, when 'from the bishops to the last of the faithful' it manifests a universal consensus in matters of faith and morals."[7] These are the famous words *infallible "in credendo."*

In the Apostolic Exhortation *Evangelii Gaudium*, I emphasized that "the people of God is holy thanks to this anointing, which makes it infallible *in credendo*,"[8] and added that "all the baptized, whatever their position in the Church or their level of instruction

[4] Saint John Paul II, *Address for the Conclusion of VI Ordinary General Assembly of the Synod of Bishops*, 29 October 1983.

[5] Cf. AAS 98 (2006), 755–779.

[6] Second Vatican Ecumenical Council, Dogmatic Constitution *Lumen Gentium* (21 November 1964) 10.

[7] Ibid., 12.

[8] Francis, Apostolic Exhortation *Evangelii Gaudium* (24 November 2013), 119.

in the faith, are agents of evangelization, and it would be insufficient to envisage a plan of evangelization to be carried out by professionals while the rest of the faithful would simply be passive recipients."[9] The *sensus fidei* prevents a rigid separation between an *Ecclesia docens* and an *Ecclesia discens*, since the flock likewise has an instinctive ability to discern the new ways that the Lord is revealing to the Church.[10]

Such was the conviction underlying my desire that the people of God should be consulted in the preparation of the two phases of the Synod on the family, as is ordinarily done with each *Lineamenta*. Certainly, a consultation of this sort would never be sufficient to perceive the *sensus fidei*. But how could we speak about the family without engaging families themselves, listening to their joys and their hopes, their sorrows and their anguish?[11] Through the answers given to the two questionnaires sent to the particular Churches, we had the opportunity at least to hear some of those families speak to issues which closely affect them and about which they have much to say.

A synodal Church is a Church which listens, which realizes that listening "is more than simply hearing."[12] It is a mutual listening in which everyone has something to learn. The faithful people, the college of bishops, the Bishop of Rome: all listening to each other, and all listening to the Holy Spirit, the "Spirit of truth" (*Jn* 14:17), in order to know what he "says to the Churches" (*Rev* 2:7).

The Synod of Bishops is the point of convergence of this listening process conducted at every level of the Church's life. The Synod process begins by listening to the people of God, which

---

[9]Ibid., 120.

[10]Cf. Francis, *Address to the Leadership of the Episcopal Conferences of Latin America during the General Coordination Meeting*, Rio de Janeiro, 28 July 2013, 5, 4; ID., *Address on the occasion of a meeting with Clergy, Consecrated Persons and members of Pastoral Councils*, Assisi, 4 October 2013.

[11]Cf. Second Vatican Ecumenical Council, Pastoral Constitution *Gaudium et Spes* (7 December 1965), 1.

[12]Apostolic Exhortation *Evangelii Gaudium*, 171.

"shares also in Christ's prophetic office,"[13] according to a principle dear to the Church of the first millennium: "*Quod omnes tangit ab omnibus tractari debet.*" The Synod process then continues by listening to the pastors. Through the Synod Fathers, the bishops act as authentic guardians, interpreters and witnesses of the faith of the whole Church, which they need to discern carefully from the changing currents of public opinion. On the eve of last year's Synod I stated: "For the Synod Fathers we ask the Holy Spirit first of all for the gift of listening: to listen to God, so that with him we may hear the cry of his people; to listen to his people until we are in harmony with the will to which God calls us."[14] The Synod process culminates in listening to the Bishop of Rome, who is called to speak as "pastor and teacher of all Christians,"[15] not on the basis of his personal convictions but as the supreme witness to the *fides totius Ecclesiae*, "the guarantor of the obedience and the conformity of the Church to the will of God, to the Gospel of Christ, and to the Tradition of the Church."[16]

The fact that the Synod always acts *cum Petro et sub Petro*—indeed, not only *cum Petro*, but also *sub Petro*—is not a limitation of freedom, but a guarantee of unity. For the Pope is, by will of the Lord, "the perpetual and visible source and foundation of the unity both of the bishops and of the whole company of the faithful."[17] Closely related to this is the concept of "*hierarchica communio*" as employed by the Second Vatican Council: the Bishops are linked to the Bishop of Rome by the bond of episcopal communion (*cum Petro*) while, at the same time, hierarchically subject to him as head of the college (*sub Petro*).[18]

---

[13]Second Vatican Ecumenical Council, Dogmatic Constitution *Lumen Gentium*, 12.

[14]Francis, *Address at the Prayer Vigil for the Synod on the Family*, 4 October 2014.

[15]First Vatican Ecumenical Council, Dogmatic Constitution *Pastor Aeternus* (18 July 1870), ch. IV: Denz. 3074. Cf. *Codex Iuris Canonici*, can. 749, § 1.

[16]Francis, *Address to the Third Extraordinary General Assembly of the Synod of Bishops*, 18 October 2014.

[17]Second Vatican Ecumenical Council, Dogmatic Constitution *Lumen Gentium*, 23. cf. First Vatican Ecumenical Council, Dogmatic Constitution *Pastor Aeternus*, Prologue: Denz. 3051.

[18]Cf. Second Vatican Ecumenical Council, Dogmatic Constitution *Lumen Gentium*,

* * *

Synodality, as a constitutive element of the Church, offers us the most appropriate interpretive framework for understanding the hierarchical ministry itself. If we understand, as Saint John Chrysostom says, that "Church and Synod are synonymous,"[19] inasmuch as the Church is nothing other than the "journeying together" of God's flock along the paths of history towards the encounter with Christ the Lord, then we understand too that, within the Church, no one can be "raised up" higher than others. On the contrary, in the Church, it is necessary that each person "lower" himself or herself, so as to serve our brothers and sisters along the way.

Jesus founded the Church by setting at her head the Apostolic College, in which the Apostle Peter is the "rock" (cf. *Mt* 16:18), the one who must confirm his brethren in the faith (cf. *Lk* 22:32). But in this Church, as in an inverted pyramid, the top is located beneath the base. Consequently, those who exercise authority are called "ministers," because, in the original meaning of the word, they are the least of all. It is in serving the people of God that each bishop becomes, for that portion of the flock entrusted to him, *vicarius Christi*,[20] the vicar of that Jesus who at the Last Supper bent down to wash the feet of the Apostles (cf. *Jn* 13:1–15). And in a similar perspective, the Successor of Peter is nothing else if not the *servus servorum Dei*.[21] Let us never forget this! For the disciples of Jesus, yesterday, today and always, the only authority is the authority of service, the only power is the power of the cross. As the Master tells us: "You know that the rulers of the Gentiles lord it over them, and their great men exercise authority over them. It shall not be so among you; but whoever would be great among you must be your servant, and whoever would be first among you

---

22; Decree *Christus Dominus* (28 October 1965), 4.

[19]Saint John Chrysostom, *Explicatio in Ps. 149*: PG 55, 493.

[20]Cf. Second Vatican Ecumenical Council, Dogmatic Constitution *Lumen Gentium*, 27.

[21]Cf. Francis, *Address to the Third Extraordinary General Assembly of the Synod of Bishops*, 18 October 2014.

must be your slave" (*Mt* 20:25–27). *It shall not be so among you*: in this expression we touch the heart of the mystery of the Church, and we receive the enlightenment necessary to understand our hierarchical service.

* * *

In a synodal Church, the Synod of Bishops is only the most evident manifestation of a dynamism of communion which inspires all ecclesial decisions.

The first level of the exercise of *synodality* is had in the particular Churches. After mentioning the noble institution of the Diocesan Synod, in which priests and laity are called to cooperate with the bishop for the good of the whole ecclesial community,[22] the *Code of Canon Law* devotes ample space to what are usually called "organs of communion" in the local Church: the presbyteral council, the college of consultors, chapters of canons and the pastoral council.[23] Only to the extent that these organizations keep connected to the "base" and start from people and their daily problems, can a synodal Church begin to take shape: these means, even when they prove wearisome, must be valued as an opportunity for listening and sharing.

The second level is that of Ecclesiastical Provinces and Ecclesiastical Regions, Particular Councils and, in a special way, Conferences of Bishops.[24] We need to reflect on how better to bring about, through these bodies, intermediary instances of *collegiality*, perhaps by integrating and updating certain aspects of the ancient ecclesiastical organization. The hope expressed by the Council that such bodies would help increase the spirit of episcopal *collegiality* has not yet been fully realized. We are still on the way, part-way there. In a synodal Church, as I have said, "it is not advisable for the Pope to take the place of local Bishops in the discernment of every issue

[22] Cf. *Codex Iuris Canonici*, cann. 460–468.
[23] Cf. ibid., cann. 495–514.
[24] Cf. ibid., cann. 431–459.

which arises in their territory. In this sense, I am conscious of the need to promote a sound 'decentralization.' "[25]

The last level is that of the universal Church. Here the Synod of Bishops, representing the Catholic episcopate, becomes an expression of *episcopal collegiality* within an entirely synodal Church.[26] Two different phrases: "episcopal collegiality" and an "entirely synodal Church." This level manifests the *collegialitas affectiva*, which can also become in certain circumstances "effective," joining the Bishops among themselves and with the Pope in solicitude for the People God.[27]

* * *

The commitment to build a synodal Church—a mission to which we are all called, each with the role entrusted him by the Lord—has significant ecumenical implications. For this reason, speaking recently to a delegation from the Patriarchate of Constantinople, I reaffirmed my conviction that "a careful examination of how, in the Church's life, the principle of synodality and the service of the one who presides are articulated, will make a significant contribution to the progress of relations between our Churches."[28]

I am persuaded that in a synodal Church, greater light can be shed on the exercise of the Petrine primacy. The Pope is not, by himself, above the Church; but within it as one of the baptized, and within the College of Bishops as a Bishop among Bishops, called at the same time—as Successor of Peter—to lead the Church of Rome which presides in charity over all the Churches.[29]

While reaffirming the urgent need to think about "a conversion

---

[25]Francis, Apostolic Exhortation *Evangelii Gaudium*, 16. cf. ibid., 32.

[26]Cf. Second Vatican Ecumenical Council, Decree *Christus Dominus*, 5; *Codex Iuris Canonici*, cann. 342–348.

[27]Cf. Saint John Paul II, Post-Synodal Apostolic Exhortation *Pastores Gregis* (16 October 2003), 8.

[28]Francis, *Address to the Delegation of the Ecumenical Patriarchate of Constantinople*, 27 June 2015.

[29]Cf. Saint Ignatius of Antioch, *Epistula ad Romanos*, Proemium: PG 5, 686.

of the papacy,"[30] I willingly repeat the words of my predecessor Pope John Paul II: "As Bishop of Rome I am fully aware [. . .] that Christ ardently desires the full and visible communion of all those Communities in which, by virtue of God's faithfulness, his Spirit dwells. I am convinced that I have a particular responsibility in this regard, above all in acknowledging the ecumenical aspirations of the majority of the Christian Communities and in heeding the request made of me to find a way of exercising the primacy which, while in no way renouncing what is essential to its mission, is nonetheless open to a new situation."[31]

Our gaze also extends to humanity as a whole. A synodal Church is like a standard lifted up among the nations (cf. *Is* 11:12) in a world which—while calling for participation, solidarity and transparency in public administration—often consigns the fate of entire peoples to the grasp of small but powerful groups. As a Church which "journeys together" with men and women, sharing the travails of history, let us cherish the dream that a rediscovery of the inviolable dignity of peoples and of the function of authority as service will also be able to help civil society to be built up in justice and fraternity, and thus bring about a more beautiful and humane world for coming generations.[32] Thank you.

---

[30]Francis, Apostolic Exhortation *Evangelii Gaudium*, 32.

[31]Saint John Paul II, Encyclical Letter *Ut Unum Sint* (25 May 1995), 95.

[32]Cf. Francis, Apostolic Exhortation *Evangelii Gaudium*, 186–192; Encyclical Letter *Laudato Si'* (24 May 2015), 156–162.

The Significance of the Synod

Conclusion of the Synod of Bishops on the Family

October 24, 2015

Dear Beatitudes, Eminences and Excellencies,
Dear Brothers and Sisters,

I would like first of all to thank the Lord, who has guided our synodal process in these years by his Holy Spirit, whose support is never lacking to the Church. . . .

I thank all of you, dear Synod Fathers, Fraternal Delegates, Auditors and Assessors, parish priests and families, for your active and fruitful participation.

And I thank all those unnamed men and women who contributed generously to the labors of this Synod by quietly working behind the scenes.

Be assured of my prayers, that the Lord will reward all of you with his abundant gifts of grace!

As I followed the labors of the Synod, I asked myself: *What will it mean for the Church to conclude this Synod devoted to the family?*

Certainly, the Synod was not about settling all the issues having to do with the family, but rather attempting to see them in the light of the Gospel and the Church's tradition and two-thousand-year history, bringing the joy of hope without falling into a facile repetition of what is obvious or has already been said.

Surely it was not about finding exhaustive solutions for all the difficulties and uncertainties which challenge and threaten the family, but rather about seeing these difficulties and uncertainties in the light of the Faith, carefully studying them and confronting them fearlessly, without burying our heads in the sand.

It was about urging everyone to appreciate the importance of the institution of the family and of marriage between a man and a woman, based on unity and indissolubility, and valuing it as the fundamental basis of society and human life.

It was about listening to and making heard the voices of the families and the Church's pastors, who came to Rome bearing on their shoulders the burdens and the hopes, the riches and the challenges of families throughout the world.

It was about showing the vitality of the Catholic Church, which is not afraid to stir dulled consciences or to soil her hands with lively and frank discussions about the family.

It was about trying to view and interpret realities, today's realities, through God's eyes, so as to kindle the flame of faith and enlighten people's hearts in times marked by discouragement, social, economic and moral crisis, and growing pessimism.

It was about bearing witness to everyone that, for the Church, the Gospel continues to be a vital source of eternal newness, against all those who would "indoctrinate" it in dead stones to be hurled at others.

It was also about laying closed hearts, which bare the closed hearts which frequently hide even behind the Church's teachings or good intentions, in order to sit in the chair of Moses and judge, sometimes with superiority and superficiality, difficult cases and wounded families.

It was about making clear that the Church is a Church of the poor in spirit and of sinners seeking forgiveness, not simply of the righteous and the holy, but rather of those who are righteous and holy precisely when they feel themselves poor sinners.

It was about trying to open up broader horizons, rising above conspiracy theories and blinkered viewpoints, so as to defend and spread the freedom of the children of God, and to transmit the beauty of Christian Newness, at times encrusted in a language which is archaic or simply incomprehensible.

In the course of this Synod, the different opinions which were freely expressed—and at times, unfortunately, not in entirely well-meaning ways—certainly led to a rich and lively dialogue; they offered a vivid image of a Church which does not simply "rubberstamp," but draws from the sources of her faith living waters to refresh parched hearts.[1]

And—apart from dogmatic questions clearly defined by the Church's Magisterium—we have also seen that what seems normal for a bishop on one continent, is considered strange and almost scandalous—almost!—for a bishop from another; what is considered a violation of a right in one society is an evident and inviolable rule in another; what for some is freedom of conscience is for others simply confusion. Cultures are in fact quite diverse, and every general principle—as I said, dogmatic questions clearly defined by the Church's magisterium—every general principle needs to be inculturated, if it is to be respected and applied.[2] The 1985 Synod, which celebrated the twentieth anniversary of the conclusion of the Second Vatican Council, spoke of *inculturation* as "the intimate transformation of authentic cultural values through their integration in Christianity, and the taking root of Christianity in the various human cultures."[3] *Inculturation* does not weaken true values, but demonstrates their true strength and authenticity, since they adapt without changing; indeed they quietly and gradually transform the different cultures.[4]

We have seen, also by the richness of our diversity, that the same challenge is ever before us: that of proclaiming the Gospel to the men and women of today, and defending the family from all ideological and individualistic assaults.

---

[1]Cf. Letter of His Holiness Pope Francis to the Grand Chancellor of the Pontifical Catholic University of Argentina on the Centenary of its Faculty of Theology, 3 March 2015.

[2]Cf. Pontifical Biblical Commission, *Fede e cultura alla luce della Bibbia. Atti della Sessione plenaria 1979 della Pontificia Commissione Biblica*, LDC, Leumann, 1981; Second Vatican Ecumenical Council, *Gaudium et Spes*, 44.

[3]*Final Relatio* (7 December 1985), *L'Osservatore Romano*, 10 December 1985, 7.

[4]"In virtue of her pastoral mission, the Church must remain ever attentive to historical changes and to the development of new ways of thinking. Not, of course, to submit to them, but rather to surmount obstacles standing in the way of accepting her counsels and directives" (Interview with Cardinal Georges Cottier, in *La Civiltà Cattolica* 3963–3964, 8 August 2015, p. 272).

And without ever falling into the danger of *relativism* or of *demonizing* others, we sought to embrace, fully and courageously, the goodness and mercy of God who transcends our every human reckoning and desires only that "all be saved" (cf. *1 Tm* 2:4). In this way we wished to experience this Synod in the context of the Extraordinary Year of Mercy which the Church is called to celebrate.

Dear Brothers and Sisters,

The Synod experience also made us better realize that the true defenders of doctrine are not those who uphold its letter, but its spirit; not ideas but people; not formulae but the gratuitousness of God's love and forgiveness. This is in no way to detract from the importance of formulae—they are necessary—or from the importance of laws and divine commandments, but rather to exalt the greatness of the true God, who does not treat us according to our merits or even according to our works but *solely* according to the boundless generosity of his Mercy (cf. *Rom* 3:21–30; *Ps* 129; *Lk* 11:47–54). It does have to do with overcoming the recurring temptations of the elder brother (cf. *Lk* 15:25–32) and the jealous laborers (cf. *Mt* 20:1–16). Indeed, it means upholding all the more the laws and commandments which were made for man and not vice versa (cf. *Mk* 2:27).

In this sense, the necessary human repentance, works and efforts take on a deeper meaning, not as the price of that salvation freely won for us by Christ on the cross, but as a response to the One who loved us first and saved us at the cost of his innocent blood, while we were still sinners (cf. *Rom* 5:6).

The Church's first duty is not to hand down condemnations or anathemas, but to proclaim God's mercy, to call to conversion, and to lead all men and women to salvation in the Lord (cf. *Jn* 12:44–50).

Blessed Paul VI expressed this eloquently: "We can imagine, then, that each of our sins, our attempts to turn our back on God, kindles in him a more intense flame of love, a desire to bring us back to himself and to his saving plan . . . God, in Christ, shows himself to be infinitely good . . . God is good. Not only in himself;

God is—let us say it with tears—good for us. He loves us, he seeks us out, he thinks of us, he knows us, he touches our hearts us and he waits for us. He will be—so to say—delighted on the day when we return and say: 'Lord, in your goodness, forgive me.' Thus our repentance becomes God's joy."[5]

Saint John Paul II also stated that "the Church lives an authentic life when she professes and proclaims mercy . . . and when she brings people close to the sources of the Savior's mercy, of which she is the trustee and dispenser."[6]

Benedict XVI, too, said: "Mercy is indeed the central nucleus of the Gospel message; it is the very name of God . . . May all that the Church says and does manifest the mercy God feels for mankind. When the Church has to recall an unrecognized truth, or a betrayed good, she always does so impelled by merciful love, so that men may have life and have it abundantly (cf. *Jn* 10:10)."[7]

In light of all this, and thanks to this time of grace which the Church has experienced in discussing the family, we feel mutually enriched. Many of us have felt the working of the Holy Spirit who is the real protagonist and guide of the Synod. For all of us, the word "family" does have the same sound as it did before the Synod, so much so that the word itself already contains the richness of the family's vocation and the significance of the labors of the Synod.[8]

---

[5]*Homily*, 23 June 1968: *Insegnamenti* VI (1968), 1177–1178.

[6]*Dives in Misericordia*, 13. He also said: "In the paschal mystery . . . God appears to us as he is: a tender-hearted Father, who does not give up in the face of his children's ingratitude and is always ready to forgive" (John Paul II, *Regina Coeli*, 23 April 1995: *Insegnamenti* XVIII, 1 [1995], 1035). So too he described resistance to mercy: "The present-day mentality, more perhaps than that of people in the past, seems opposed to a God of mercy, and in fact tends to exclude from life and to remove from the human heart the very idea of mercy. The word and the concept of 'mercy' seem to cause uneasiness . . ." (*Dives in Misericordia* [30 November 1980] 2).

[7]*Regina Coeli*, 30 March 2008: *Insegnamenti* IV, 1 (2008), 489–490. Speaking of the power of mercy, he stated: "it is mercy that sets a limit to evil. In it is expressed God's special nature—his holiness, the power of truth and of love" (*Homily* on Divine Mercy Sunday, 15 April 2007: *Insegnamenti* III, 1 [2007], 667).

[8]An acrostic look at the word "family" [Italian: "*famiglia*"] can help us summarize the Church's mission as the task of: Forming new generations to experience love seriously, not as an individualistic search for a pleasure then to be discarded, and to

In effect, for the Church *to conclude* the Synod means *to return* to our true "journeying together" in bringing to every part of the world, to every diocese, to every community and every situation, the light of the Gospel, the embrace of the Church and the support of God's mercy!

Thank you!

---

believe once again in true, fruitful and lasting love as the sole way of emerging from ourselves and being open to others, leaving loneliness behind, living according to God's will, finding fulfilment, realizing that marriage is "an experience which reveals God's love, defending the sacredness of life, every life, defending the unity and indissolubility of the conjugal bond as a sign of God's grace and of the human person's ability to love seriously" (*Homily* for the Opening Mass of the Synod, 4 October 2015: *L'Osservatore Romano*, 5–6 October 2015, p. 7) and, furthermore, enhancing marriage preparation as a means of providing a deeper understanding of the Christian meaning of the sacrament of Matrimony; Approaching others, since a Church closed in on herself is a dead Church, while a Church which does leave her own precincts behind in order to seek, embrace and lead others to Christ is a Church which betrays her very mission and calling; Manifesting and bringing God's mercy to families in need; to the abandoned, to the neglected elderly, to children pained by the separation of their parents, to poor families struggling to survive, to sinners knocking on our doors and those who are far away, to the differently abled, to all those hurting in soul and body, and to couples torn by grief, sickness, death or persecution; Illuminating consciences often assailed by harmful and subtle dynamics which even attempt to replace God the Creator, dynamics which must be unmasked and resisted in full respect for the dignity of each person; Gaining and humbly rebuilding trust in the Church, which has been gravely weakened as a result of the conduct and sins of her children—sadly, the counter-witness of scandals committed in the Church by some clerics have damaged her credibility and obscured the brightness of her saving message; Laboring intensely to sustain and encourage those many strong and faithful families which, in the midst of their daily struggles, continue to give a great witness of fidelity to the Church's teachings and the Lord's commandments; Inventing renewed programs of pastoral care for the family based on the Gospel and respectful of cultural differences, pastoral care which is capable of communicating the Good News in an attractive and positive manner and helping banish from young hearts the fear of making definitive commitments, pastoral care which is particularly attentive to children, who are the real victims of broken families, pastoral care which is innovative and provides a suitable preparation for the sacrament of Matrimony, rather than so many programs which seem more of a formality than training for a lifelong commitment; Aiming to love unconditionally all families, particularly those experiencing difficulties, since no family should feel alone or excluded from the Church's loving embrace, and the real scandal is a fear of love and of showing that love concretely.

Looking to God's People

Letter to Cardinal Marc Ouellet, President of the Pontifical Commission

March 19, 2016

Your Eminence,

At the end of the meeting of the Commission for Latin America and the Caribbean, I had the opportunity to meet with all those attending the assembly, during which there was an exchange of ideas and impressions concerning the public participation of the laity in the life of our peoples.

Now I would like to recount what was shared in that encounter and to follow it up with a reflection on those days, so that the spirit of discernment and reflection "doesn't fall into the void"; so that it may help us and continue to encourage us to better serve the faithful Holy People of God.

It is precisely this image from which I would like to begin our reflection on the public activity of the laity in our Latin American context. To evoke the faithful Holy People of God is to evoke the horizon to which we are called to look and reflect. It is the faithful Holy People of God to whom as pastors we are continually called to look, protect, accompany, support and serve. A father cannot conceive of himself without his children. He may be an excellent worker, a professional, a husband or friend, but what makes him a father figure are his children. The same goes for us, we are pastors. A shepherd cannot conceive of himself without his flock, whom he is called to serve. The pastor is pastor of a people, and he serves this people from within. Many times he goes ahead to lead the way; at other times he retraces his steps lest anyone be left behind;

and, not infrequently, he stands in the middle to know the pulse of the people.

Looking to the faithful Holy People of God, and feeling ourselves an integral part of the same, places us in life and thus in the themes that we treat, in a different way. This helps us not to fall into reflections that, in themselves, may be very good but which end up homologizing the life of our people or theorizing to the point that considerations end by prohibiting action. Looking continually at the People of God saves us from certain declarationist nominalisms (slogans) that are fine phrases but that are unable to sustain the life our communities. For example, I now recall the famous phrase: "the hour of the laity has come," but it seems the clock has stopped.

Looking at the People of God is remembering that we all enter the Church as lay people. The first sacrament, which seals our identity forever, and of which we should always be proud, is Baptism. Through Baptism and by the anointing of the Holy Spirit, (the faithful) "are consecrated as a spiritual house and a holy priesthood" (*Lumen Gentium,* n. 10). Our first and fundamental consecration is rooted in our Baptism. No one has been baptized a priest or a bishop. They baptized us as lay people and it is the indelible sign that no one can ever erase. It does us good to remember that the Church is not an elite of priests, of consecrated men, of bishops, but that everyone forms the faithful Holy People of God. To forget this carries many risks and distortions in our own experience, be they personal or communitary, of the ministry that the Church has entrusted to us. We are, as firmly emphasized by the Second Vatican Council, the People of God, whose identity is "the dignity and freedom of the sons of God, in whose hearts the Holy Spirit dwells as in His temple" (*Lumen Gentium*, n. 9). The faithful Holy People of God is anointed with the grace of the Holy Spirit, and thus, as we reflect, think, evaluate, discern, we must be very attentive to this anointing.

At the same time I must add another element that I consider the fruit of a mistaken way of living out the ecclesiology proposed by Vatican II. We cannot reflect on the theme of the laity while ignoring one of the greatest distortions that Latin America has to confront—and to which I ask you to devote special attention—clericalism. This approach not only nullifies the character of Christians, but also tends to diminish and undervalue the baptismal grace that the Holy Spirit has placed in the heart of our people. Clericalism leads to homologization of the laity; treating the laity as "representative" limits the diverse initiatives and efforts and, dare I say, the necessary boldness to enable the Good News of the Gospel to be brought to all areas of the social and above all political sphere. Clericalism, far from giving impetus to various contributions and proposals, gradually extinguishes the prophetic flame to which the entire Church is called to bear witness in the heart of her peoples. Clericalism forgets that the visibility and sacramentality of the Church belong to all the People of God (cf. *Lumen Gentium*, nn. 9–14), not only to the few chosen and enlightened.

There is a very interesting phenomenon produced in our Latin America that I would like to quote here: I believe it to be one of the few areas in which the People of God is free from the influence of clericalism. I am referring to popular devotion. It has been one of the few areas in which the people (including its pastors) and the Holy Spirit have been able to meet without the clericalism that seeks to control and restrain God's anointing of his own. We know that popular devotion, as Paul VI aptly wrote in his Apostolic Exhortation *Evangelii Nuntiandi,* "certainly has its limits. It is often subject to penetration by many distortions of religion," but, he continued, "If it is well oriented, above all by a pedagogy of evangelization, it is rich in values. It manifests a thirst for God which only the simple and poor can know. It makes people capable of generosity and sacrifice even to the point of heroism, when it is a question of manifesting belief. It involves an acute awareness of profound attributes of God: fatherhood, providence, loving and constant presence. It engenders interior attitudes rarely observed to the same degree elsewhere: patience, the sense of the cross in daily life, detachment, openness to others, devotion. By reason of these aspects, we readily call it 'popular piety,' that is, religion of the people, rather than religiosity. . . . When it is well oriented, this popular religiosity call be more and more for multitudes of our people a true encounter with God in Jesus Christ" (n. 48). Pope Paul VI used an expression that I consider fundamental, the faith of our people, their guidelines, research, aspirations, yearning. When they manage to listen and orient themselves, they are able to manifest a genuine presence of the Spirit. Let us trust in our People, in their memory and in their 'sense of smell,' let us trust that the Holy Spirit acts in and with our People and that this Spirit is not merely the "property" of the ecclesial hierarchy.

I took this example of popular devotion as a hermeneutic key that can help us to better understand the action that is generated when the faithful Holy People of God pray and act. An action that does not remain tied to the intimate sphere of the person but which, on the contrary, is transformed into culture; "an evangelized popular culture contains values of faith and solidarity capable of encouraging the development of a more just and believing society, and possesses a particular wisdom which ought to be gratefully acknowledged" (*Evangelii Gaudium*, n. 68).

From here then, we can ask ourselves: what does it mean that lay people are working in public life?

Nowadays many of our cities have become true places of survival. Places in which the throw-away culture seems to have taken over, leaving little room for hope. There we find our brothers and sisters, immersed in these struggles, with their families, who seek not only to survive but among the contradictions and injustices, seek the Lord and long to bear witness to him. What does the fact that lay people are working in public life mean for us pastors? It means finding a way to be able to encourage, accompany and inspire all attempts and efforts that are being made today in order to keep hope and faith alive in a world full of contradictions, especially for the poor, especially with the poorest. It means, as pastors, committing ourselves among our people and, with our people, supporting their faith and hope. Opening doors, working with them, dreaming with them, reflecting and above all praying with them. "We need to look at our cities"—and thus all areas where the life of our people unfolds—"with a contemplative gaze, a gaze of faith which sees God dwelling in their homes, in their streets and squares. . . . He dwells among them, fostering solidarity, fraternity, and the desire for goodness, truth and justice. This presence must not be contrived but found, uncovered. God does not hide himself from those who seek him with a sincere heart" (*Evangelii Gaudium*, n. 71). It is not the pastor to tell lay people what they must do and say; they know this better than we do. It is not for the pastor to establish what the faithful must say in various settings. As pastors, united with our people, it does us good to ask ourselves how we are encouraging and promoting charity and fraternity, the desire for good, for truth and for justice; how we can ensure that corruption does not settle in our hearts.

Often we have given in to the temptation of thinking that committed lay people are those dedicated to the works of the Church and/or the matters of the parish or the diocese, and we have reflected little on how to accompany baptized people in their public and daily life; on how in their daily activities, with the responsibilities they have, they are committed as Christians in public life. Without realizing it, we have generated a lay elite, believing that committed lay people are only those who work in the matters "of priests," and we have forgotten, overlooked, the believers who very often burn out their hope in the daily struggle to live the faith. These are the situations that clericalism fails to notice, because it is more concerned with dominating spaces than with generating initiatives. Therefore we must recognize that lay people—through their reality, through their identity, for they are immersed in the heart of social, public and political life, participate in cultural forms that are constantly generated—need new forms of organization and of celebration of the faith. The current pace is so different (I do not say better or worse) than what we were living 30 years ago! "This challenges us to imagine innovative spaces and possibilities for prayer and communion which are more attractive and meaningful for city dwellers" (*Evangelii Gaudium*, n. 73). It is illogical and therefore impossible to think that we as pastors should have the monopoly on solutions for the multitude of challenges that contemporary life presents us. On the contrary, we must be on the side of our people, accompanying them in their search and encouraging the imagination capable of responding to the current set of problems. We must do this by discerning with our people and never for our people or without our people. As St Ignatius would say, "in line with the necessities of place, time and person." In other words, not uniformly. We cannot give general directives in order to organize the People of God within its public life. Inculturation is a process that we pastors are called to inspire, encouraging people to live their faith where and with whom they are. Inculturation is learning to discover how a determinate portion of the people today, in the historical here and now, live, celebrate and proclaim their faith. With a particular identity and on the basis of the problems that must be faced, as well as with all the reasons they have to rejoice. Inculturation is the work of artisans and not of a factory with a production line dedicated to "manufacturing Christian worlds or spaces."

There are two memories that should be asked to be safeguarded in our people. The memory of Jesus Christ and the memory of our forebears. The faith we have received was a gift that came to us in many cases from the hands of our mothers, from our grandmothers. They were the living memory of Jesus Christ within our homes. It was in the silence of family life that most of us learned to pray, to love, to live the faith. It was within family life, which then took on the shape of parish, school, community, that the faith came into our life and became flesh. It was this simple faith that accompanied us often in the many vicissitudes of the journey. To lose our memory is to uproot ourselves from where we came and therefore is also not even knowing where we are going. This is fundamental, when we uproot a lay person from his faith, from that of his origins; when we uproot him from the faithful Holy People of God, we uproot him from his baptismal identity and thus we deprive him of the grace of the Holy Spirit. The same happens to us when we uproot ourselves as pastors from our people, we become lost. Our role, our joy, a pastor's joy, lies precisely in helping and in encouraging, as many have done before us: mothers, grandmothers and fathers, history's real protagonists. Not through our concession of good will, but by right and actual statute. Lay people are part of the faithful Holy People of God and thus are the protagonists of the Church and of the world; we are called to serve them, not to be served by them.

In my recent journey on Mexican soil, I had the opportunity to be alone with our Mother, allowing myself to be looked at by her. In that space of prayer, I was also able to present my filial heart to her. In that moment you too were there with your communities. In that moment of prayer, I asked that Mary never cease to support, as she did with the first community, the faith of our people. May the Blessed Virgin intercede for you, protect you and accompany you always!

Future Horizons

From an Interview with Guillaume Goubert and Sébastien Maillard

La Croix, May 17, 2016

In the post-synodal exhortation [*Amoris laetitia*, April 2016], I have tried to respect the Synod as much as possible. You will not find in it canonical clarifications of what one can or should do or not do. It is a calm and peaceful reflection on the beauty of love, how to raise children, prepare for marriage, etc. It values responsibilities that could be accompanied by the Pontifical Council for the Laity in the form of guidelines.

Beyond this process, we need to think about true synodality, at least what Catholic synodality means. The bishops are *cum Petro, sub Petro* [with Peter's successor and under Peter's successor]. This differs from Orthodox synodality and that of the Greek Catholic Churches, where the patriarch counts as a single vote.

The Second Vatican Council gives an ideal of synodal and episcopal communion. This still needs to be developed, even at the parish level in terms of what is prescribed. There are parishes that still do not have a pastoral council or a council for economic affairs, even though these are obligations under canon law. Synodality is also relevant at this level.

Synod to Say: "We Young People Are Here!"

Prayer Vigil in Preparation of World Youth Day

PAPAL BASILICA OF ST. MARY MAJOR, APRIL 8, 2017

Dear Young Friends,

Thank you for coming! This evening marks a double beginning. It is the beginning of the *journey towards the Synod*, which has a very long name—"*Young People, the Faith and Vocational Discernment,*" but we can just call it the Synod of Young People. That way it is easier to understand! It is also a second beginning, the beginning of our *journey to Panama*. The Archbishop of Panama is with us, and I greet him warmly.

We have listened to the Gospel, prayed, sung and brought flowers to the Madonna, our Mother. We also brought the World Youth Day cross, which has come from Kraków and will be handed over tomorrow to the young people from Panama. From Kraków to Panama, with the Synod in between. A Synod from which no young person should feel excluded!

Some people say: "Let's hold the Synod for young Catholics, for those belonging to Catholic groups; that way it will be better." No! The Synod is meant to be the Synod *for* and *of* all young people. Young people are its protagonists. "But even young people who consider themselves agnostics?" Yes! "Even young people whose faith is lukewarm?" Yes! "Even young people who no longer go to Church?" Yes! "Even young people who—I don't know if there are any here, maybe one or two—consider themselves atheists?" Yes! This is the Synod of young people and we want to *listen to one another.* Every young person has something to say to others. He or she has something to say to adults, something to say to priests, sisters, bishops and even the Pope. All of us need to listen to you!

Let's think back to Kraków; the cross is a reminder. There I said two things, perhaps some of you will remember. First, it is not good to see a young person already retired at twenty! Second, it is also not good to see a young person spending his or her life on a couch. Isn't this the truth? We need *young people who are neither retired nor couch potatoes!* We need young people who are on the road and moving forward, at each other's side but looking ahead to the future!

In the Gospel (cf. *Lk* 1:39–45) we heard how Mary receives that grace, that immense *vocation* of bringing God's gift to us. The Gospel tells us that after hearing that her elderly cousin was expecting a child and needed help, Mary sets out in haste to help her. She hurries! The world today needs young people who "hurry," who don't get tired of hurrying. We need young people who feel a call, who feel that life offers them *a mission*. Young people who, as Maria Lisa (a young religious Sister) said so often in her testimony, are *on the go*. Maria Lisa shared her experience with us: it was an experience of being on the go. We need young people on the go. The world can change only if young people are on the go.

But this is the tragedy of the world today, and of young people today, that *young people are often discarded.* They don't have work, they don't have an ideal to pursue, they lack education and they lack integration. So many young people have to flee, to migrate to other lands. Young people today, it is painful to say, are often discarded. We cannot tolerate this! We have to hold this Synod to say: "We young people are here!" And we are going to Panama to say: "We young people are here, on the march, and we don't want to be discarded! We have something of value to give!

While Pompeo was talking (in the second testimony), I was thinking that twice he was almost at the point of being discarded—when he was eight and again when he was eighteen. But he made it: he was able to pick himself up. Life, when we look up always surprises us. Maria Lisa said this too. They both said this.

We are on the march, towards the Synod and towards Panama. And this march has its risks, but when young people don't take risks, they are already old. We have to take risks.

Maria Lisa said that after receiving the sacrament of Confirmation she fell away from the Church. You all know that here in Italy the sacrament of Confirmation is called the "sacrament of farewell"! After Confirmation, people stop going to church. Why? Because so many young people don't know what to do. But Maria Lisa never stopped, she kept walking: at times along dark ways, poorly-lit ways, without ideals or with ideals that she didn't quite understand; but in the end she too made it. As young people, you have to take a risk in life. You have to prepare for tomorrow today. The future is in your hands.

In the Synod, the entire Church wants to listen to young people: to what they are thinking, to what they want, to what they criticize and to what they are sorry for. Everything. The Church needs lots more springtime, and springtime is the season of the young.

I want to invite you to make this journey, this march towards the Synod and towards Panama, and to make it with joy, with your aspirations, without fear, without shame, and to make it courageously. Courage is needed. But also the effort to appreciate the beauty of little things, as Pompeo said: the beauty of everyday life. Be grateful for life, don't ever lose this ability. Be thankful for what you are: "This is how I am, thank you!" So often in life, we waste time asking ourselves: "Who am I?" You can keep asking, "Who am I?" for the rest of your lives. But the real question is: "*For whom* am I?" Like Our Lady, who could ask: *"For whom, for what person, am I,"* here and now? She answers, "For my cousin," and off she goes. "For whom am I?" not "Who am I?" The answer to that second question comes later; it is a question that has to be asked, but first you have to ask *why*: why you do something, something for your entire life, something that makes you *think*, makes you *feel*, makes you *work*. There are these three languages: the language of the *mind*, the language of the *heart*, and the language of the *hands*. Never stop moving ahead.

There is something else I want to tell you. The Synod will not be a "chat room." World Youth Day will not be a chat room, or a form of entertainment, or a nice happy experience from which you can then move on. No! *Concreteness!* Life demands concreteness of us. In this liquid culture, we need concreteness, and concreteness is your vocation.

Now I would like to conclude . . . I had a written speech, but after seeing you, after listening to the testimonies, I thought I should say all the things I just told you. There are going to be times when you don't understand, dark times, painful times, but also wonderful times, times of darkness and times of light . . . But I want to make one thing clear. We live in the present. At my age, people are getting ready to leave the scene . . . right? Who can be sure about life? Nobody. At your age, you have the future ahead of you. Life holds out a mission to young people today; the Church holds out a mission, and I would like to entrust you with this mission. It is to go back and talk to your grandparents. Today more than ever we need this bridge, this dialogue, between grandparents and grandchildren, between the young and the elderly. The prophet Joel makes this prophecy: "Your old men shall dream dreams, and your young men shall see visions" (2.28). In other words, the young will make things happen because of their vision. So this is the task I am giving you in the name of the Church. *Talk to older people.* You may say: "But it's boring . . . They are always talking about the same things . . ." No! Listen to older people, talk to them, ask them questions. Make them dream, and from those dreams take what you need to move forward, so that you can have a vision and make that vision concrete. This is your mission today. This is the mission the Church gives you today.

Dear young friends, be courageous! You may say: "But Father, I have sinned, I fall so often!" I think of an Alpine song, a lovely song that mountaineers sing: "In the art of scaling a mountain, the important thing is not that you fall; it is that you get up and keep going!" Have you fallen? Get up and keep moving. But think about the dreams your grandfather or grandmother had, make them talk about them, take those things and build the bridge to the future. This is the task and the mission the Church is giving you today.

Thank you so much for your courage and now . . . off to Panama! I don't know whether I will be there, but the Pope will be there! And the Pope in Panama will ask you this question: "Did you talk to older people? Did you take the dreams of the elderly and make them visions? Are you making them happen? This is your task. May the Lord bless you. Pray for me, and together let us prepare for the Synod and for Panama. Thank you.

To Let the Truth Shine in Our Lives

Letter to the Bishops of Chile Following the Report of Archbishop Charles J. Scicluna

April 8, 2018

Dear Bishops of Chile, Dear Brothers in the Episcopate,

The receipt last week of the latest documents that complete the report consigned to me by my two Special Envoys to Chile on March 20, 2018, totaling more than 2,300 pages, has moved me to write this letter. I assure you of my prayers and I would like to share with you the conviction that the present difficulties are also an opportunity to re-establish trust in the Church, trust shattered by our errors and sins, and to heal some wounds that continue to bleed in the whole of Chilean society.

Without faith and without prayer, fraternity is impossible. Therefore, on this Second Sunday of Easter, on the day of mercy, I offer you this reflection in the hope that each of you may accompany me on the inner journey that I have been undertaking in recent weeks, so that the Spirit may guide us with his gift and not our interests or, even worse, our wounded pride.

At times, when similar evils have marred our spirit and cast us into the world weak, fearful, shielded in our comfortable "winter palaces," God's love comes to meet us and to cleanse our intentions so that we may love as free, mature and discerning men. When the communications media embarrass us by presenting a Church almost always under a new moon, bereft of the light of the Sun of justice (Saint Ambrose, *Hexameron* iv, 8:32) and we are tempted to doubt the Paschal victory of the Risen One, I believe that as Saint Thomas we must not be afraid of doubt (Jn 20:25), but must fear the insistent longing to see without trusting the witness of those who have heard the most beautiful promise from the Lord's lips (Mt 28:20).

Today I ask you to speak not of certainties, but of the one thing that the Lord allows us to experience every day: joy, peace, forgiveness of our sins and the action of his grace.

In this regard, I would like to express my gratitude to Archbishop Charles Scicluna of Malta and Msgr. Jorge Bertomeu Farnós, official of the Congregation for the Doctrine of Faith, for the amount of work involved in the calm and empathetic listening to the 64 depositions they collected recently both in New York and in Santiago de Chile. I sent them to listen from the heart and with humility. Afterwards, when they delivered the report to me and, especially, in their juridical and pastoral assessment of the information gathered, they acknowledged that they had felt overwhelmed by the pain of so many victims of serious abuses of conscience and of power and, in particular, of sexual abuse committed against minors by various consecrated people in your country, which, denied at the time, robbed them of their innocence.

As pastors we must express heartfelt and cordial gratitude to those who, with honesty, courage and *sensus Ecclesiae*, requested to meet my Envoys and showed them the wounds in their very soul. Archbishop Scicluna and Msgr. Bertomeu told me that, with impressive maturity, respect and amiability, several bishops, priests, deacons, laymen and laywomen of Santiago and Osorno went to Holy Name Parish in New York or to Sotero Sanz, in Providencia.

Moreover, in the days following the special mission, there were witnesses to another fact worth keeping in mind for other occasions, since not only was the climate of confidentiality established during the Visit maintained, but at no time did anyone succumb to the temptation to turn that delicate mission into a media circus. In this respect, I would like to thank the various organizations and means of communication for their professionalism in dealing with this most delicate case, respecting the right of citizens to information and the good reputation of the declarants.

Now, after a careful reading of the acts of this "special mission," I believe I can state that all of the collected statements speak in a straightforward manner, without additives or sugarcoating, of many lives crucified, and I confess that this causes me sorrow and shame.

Taking all of this into account, I write to you, gathered in the 115th Plenary Assembly, in order to humbly request your cooperation and assistance in discerning the measures that must be adopted in the short, medium and long term in order to restore ecclesial communion in Chile, in order to remedy the scandal to the extent possible, and re-establish justice.

I intend to summon you to Rome in order to discuss the conclusions of the aforementioned visit and my own conclusions. I have envisioned this encounter as a fraternal moment, with neither prejudice nor preconceived ideas, with the sole aim of making the truth shine forth in our lives. As to the date, I ask the Secretary of the Episcopal Conference to suggest a convenient time.

With regard to myself, I recognize, and I would like you to convey this faithfully, that I have made serious errors in the assessment and perception of the situation, in particular through the lack of reliable and balanced information. I now beg the forgiveness of all those whom I have offended and I hope to be able to do so personally, in the coming weeks, in the meetings that I will have with representatives of the people interviewed.

"Abide in me" (Jn 15:4): these words of the Lord continually resonate in these days. They speak of personal relationships, of communion, of fraternity that attracts and summons. United to Christ as branches to the vine, I invite you to instill in your prayers in the coming days a magnanimity that may prepare us for the above-mentioned meeting and allow us then to transform into concrete acts all that we will have reflected upon. Now more than ever we cannot fall back into the temptation of verbosity and maintain "universal" themes. In these days, let us look to Christ. Let us look to his life and his gestures, especially when he shows he is compassionate and merciful to those who have done wrong. Let us love truth; let us ask for wisdom of heart and allow ourselves to convert.

I look forward to hearing from you and, asking Bishop Santiago Silva Retamales, President of the Episcopal Conference of Chile, to publish the present letter as soon as possible, I impart to you my blessing and I ask you, please, to never cease praying for me.

A Task That Involves and Concerns All of God's People

Letter to the People of God

August 20, 2018

"If one member suffers, all suffer together with it" (*1 Cor* 12:26). These words of Saint Paul forcefully echo in my heart as I acknowledge once more the suffering endured by many minors due to sexual abuse, the abuse of power and the abuse of conscience perpetrated by a significant number of clerics and consecrated persons. Crimes that inflict deep wounds of pain and powerlessness, primarily among the victims, but also in their family members and in the larger community of believers and nonbelievers alike. Looking back to the past, no effort to beg pardon and to seek to repair the harm done will ever be sufficient. Looking ahead to the future, no effort must be spared to create a culture able to prevent such situations from happening, but also to prevent the possibility of their being covered up and perpetuated. The pain of the victims and their families is also our pain, and so it is urgent that we once more reaffirm our commitment to ensure the protection of minors and of vulnerable adults.

1. If one member suffers. . .

In recent days, a report was made public which detailed the experiences of at least a thousand survivors, victims of sexual abuse, the abuse of power and of conscience at the hands of priests over a period of approximately seventy years. Even though it can be said that most of these cases belong to the past, nonetheless as time goes on we have come to know the pain of many of the victims. We have realized that these wounds never disappear and that they require us forcefully to condemn these atrocities and join forces in uprooting this culture of death; these wounds never go away. The heart-wrenching pain of these victims, which cries out to heaven, was long ignored, kept quiet or silenced. But their outcry was more powerful than all the measures meant to silence it, or sought even to resolve it by decisions that increased its gravity by falling into complicity. The Lord heard that cry and once again showed us on which side he stands. Mary's song is not mistaken and continues quietly to echo throughout history. For the Lord remembers the promise he made to our fathers: "he has scattered the proud in their conceit; he has cast down the mighty from their thrones and lifted up the lowly; he has filled the hungry with good things, and the rich he has sent away empty" (*Lk* 1:51–53). We feel shame when we realize that our style of life has denied, and continues to deny, the words we recite.

With shame and repentance, we acknowledge as an ecclesial community that we were not where we should have been, that we did not act in a timely manner, realizing the magnitude and the gravity of the damage done to so many lives. We showed no care for the little ones; we abandoned them. I make my own the words of the then Cardinal Ratzinger when, during the Way of the Cross composed for Good Friday 2005, he identified with the cry of pain of so many victims and exclaimed: "How much filth there is in the Church, and even among those who, in the priesthood, ought to belong entirely to [Christ]! How much pride, how much self-complacency! Christ's betrayal by his disciples, their unworthy reception of his body and blood, is certainly the greatest suffering endured by the Redeemer; it pierces his heart. We can only call to him from the depths of our hearts: *Kyrie eleison*—Lord, save us! (cf. *Mt* 8:25)" (Ninth Station).

2. . . . all suffer together with it

The extent and the gravity of all that has happened requires coming to grips with this reality in a comprehensive and communal way. While it is important and necessary on every journey of conversion to acknowledge the truth of what has happened, in itself this is not enough. Today we are challenged as the People of God to take on the pain of our brothers and sisters wounded in their flesh and in their spirit. If, in the past, the response was one of omission, today we want solidarity, in the deepest and most challenging sense, to become our way of forging present and future history. And this in an environment where conflicts, tensions, and above all the victims of every type of abuse can encounter an outstretched hand to protect them and rescue them from their pain (cf. *Evangelii Gaudium*, 228). Such solidarity demands that we in turn condemn whatever endangers the integrity of any person. A solidarity that summons us to fight all forms of corruption, especially spiritual corruption. The latter is "a comfortable and self-satisfied form of blindness. Everything then appears acceptable: deception, slander, egotism and other subtle forms of self-centeredness, for 'even Satan disguises himself as an angel of light' (*2 Cor* 11:14)" (*Gaudete et Exsultate*, 165). Saint Paul's exhortation to suffer with those who suffer is the best antidote against all our attempts to repeat the words of Cain: "Am I my brother's keeper?" (*Gen* 4:9).

I am conscious of the effort and work being carried out in various parts of the world to come up with the necessary means to ensure the safety and protection of the integrity of children and of vulnerable adults, as well as implementing zero tolerance and ways of making all those who perpetrate or cover up these crimes accountable. We have delayed in applying these actions and sanctions that are so necessary, yet I am confident that they will help to guarantee a greater culture of care in the present and future.

Together with those efforts, every one of the baptized should feel involved in the ecclesial and social change that we so greatly need. This change calls for a personal and communal conversion that makes us see things as the Lord does. For as Saint John Paul II liked to say: "If we have truly started out anew from the contemplation of Christ, we must learn to see him especially in the faces of those with whom he wished to be identified" (*Novo Millennio Ineunte*, 49). To see things as the Lord does, to be where the Lord wants us to be, to experience a conversion of heart in his presence. To do so, prayer and penance will help. I invite the entire holy faithful

People of God to a *penitential exercise of prayer and fasting*, following the Lord's command.[1] This can awaken our conscience and arouse our solidarity and commitment to a culture of care that says "never again" to every form of abuse.

It is impossible to think of a conversion of our activity as a Church that does not include the active participation of all the members of God's People. Indeed, whenever we have tried to replace, or silence, or ignore, or reduce the People of God to small elites, we end up creating communities, projects, theological approaches, spiritualties and structures without roots, without memory, without faces, without bodies and ultimately, without lives.[2] This is clearly seen in a peculiar way of understanding the Church's authority, one common in many communities where sexual abuse and the abuse of power and conscience have occurred. Such is the case with clericalism, an approach that "not only nullifies the character of Christians, but also tends to diminish and undervalue the baptismal grace that the Holy Spirit has placed in the heart of our people."[3] Clericalism, whether fostered by priests themselves or by lay persons, leads to an excision in the ecclesial body that supports and helps to perpetuate many of the evils that we are condemning today. To say "no" to abuse is to say an emphatic "no" to all forms of clericalism.

It is always helpful to remember that "in salvation history, the Lord saved one people. We are never completely ourselves unless we belong to a people. That is why no one is saved alone, as an isolated individual. Rather, God draws us to himself, taking into account the complex fabric of interpersonal relationships present in the human community. God wanted to enter into the life and history of a people" (*Gaudete et Exsultate*, 6). Consequently, the only way that we have to respond to this evil that has darkened

[1]"But this kind [of demon] does not come out except by prayer and fasting" (*Mt* 17:21).

[2]Cf. *Letter to the Pilgrim People of God in Chile* (31 May 2018).

[3]*Letter to Cardinal Marc Ouellet, President of the Pontifical Commission for Latin America* (19 March 2016).

so many lives is to experience it as a task regarding all of us as the People of God. This awareness of being part of a people and a shared history will enable us to acknowledge our past sins and mistakes with a penitential openness that can allow us to be renewed from within. Without the active participation of all the Church's members, everything being done to uproot the culture of abuse in our communities will not be successful in generating the necessary dynamics for sound and realistic change. The penitential dimension of fasting and prayer will help us as God's People to come before the Lord and our wounded brothers and sisters as sinners imploring forgiveness and the grace of shame and conversion. In this way, we will come up with actions that can generate resources attuned to the Gospel. For "whenever we make the effort to return to the source and to recover the original freshness of the Gospel, new avenues arise, new paths of creativity open up, with different forms of expression, more eloquent signs and words with new meaning for today's world" (*Evangelii Gaudium*, 11).

It is essential that we, as a Church, be able to acknowledge and condemn, with sorrow and shame, the atrocities perpetrated by consecrated persons, clerics, and all those entrusted with the mission of watching over and caring for those most vulnerable. Let us beg forgiveness for our own sins and the sins of others. An awareness of sin helps us to acknowledge the errors, the crimes and the wounds caused in the past and allows us, in the present, to be more open and committed along a journey of renewed conversion.

Likewise, penance and prayer will help us to open our eyes and our hearts to other people's sufferings and to overcome the thirst for power and possessions that are so often the root of those evils. May fasting and prayer open our ears to the hushed pain felt by children, young people and the disabled. A fasting that can make us hunger and thirst for justice and impel us to walk in the truth, supporting all the judicial measures that may be necessary. A fasting that shakes us up and leads us to be committed in truth and charity with all men and women of good will, and with society in general, to combatting all forms of the abuse of power, sexual abuse and the abuse of conscience.

In this way, we can show clearly our calling to be "a sign and instrument of communion with God and of the unity of the entire human race" (*Lumen Gentium*, 1).

"If one member suffers, all suffer together with it," said Saint Paul. By an attitude of prayer and penance, we will become attuned as individuals and as a community to this exhortation, so that we may grow in the gift of compassion, in justice, prevention and reparation. Mary chose to stand at the foot of her Son's cross. She did so unhesitatingly, standing firmly by Jesus' side. In this way, she reveals the way she lived her entire life. When we experience the desolation caused by these ecclesial wounds, we will do well, with Mary, "to insist more upon prayer," seeking to grow all the more in love and fidelity to the Church (Saint Ignatius of Loyola, *Spiritual Exercises*, 319). She, the first of the disciples, teaches all of us as disciples how we are to halt before the sufferings of the innocent, without excuses or cowardice. To look to Mary is to discover the model of a true follower of Christ.

May the Holy Spirit grant us the grace of conversion and the interior anointing needed to express before these crimes of abuse our compunction and our resolve courageously to combat them.

Listening to the People of God

Apostolic Constitution,
Episcopalis Communio *(nns. 5–8)*
On the Synod of Bishops

SEPTEMBER 15, 2018

For these reasons, since the beginning of my Petrine ministry, I have paid special attention to the Synod of Bishops, confident that it can experience "further development so as to do even more to promote dialogue and cooperation among Bishops themselves and between them and the Bishop of Rome."[1] Underpinning this work of renewal must be the firm conviction that all Bishops are appointed for the service of the holy People of God, to whom they themselves belong through the sacrament of Baptism.

It is certainly true, as the Second Vatican Council teaches, that "when Bishops engage in teaching, in communion with the Roman Pontiff, they deserve respect from all, as the witnesses of divine and catholic truth; the faithful must agree with the judgment of their Bishop on faith and morals, which he delivers in the name of Christ; they must give it their adherence with religious assent of the mind."[2] But it is also true that "for every Bishop the life of the Church and life in the Church is the condition for exercising his mission to teach."[3]

Hence the Bishop is both teacher and disciple. He is a teacher when, endowed with the special assistance of the Holy Spirit, he

---

[1]Address to Members of the XIII Ordinary Council of the General Secretariat of the Synod of Bishops (13 June 2013).

[2]*Lumen Gentium*, 25.

[3]Post-Synodal Apostolic Exhortation *Pastores Gregis*, 28.

proclaims to the faithful the word of truth in the name of Christ, head and shepherd. But he is a disciple when, knowing that the Spirit has been bestowed upon every baptized person, he listens to the voice of Christ speaking through the entire People of God, making it "infallible *in credendo*."[4] Indeed, "the universal body made up of the faithful, whom the Holy One has anointed (cf. *1 Jn* 2:20, 27), is incapable of erring in belief. This is a property which belongs to the people as a whole; a supernatural sense of faith is the means by which they make this property manifest, when 'from Bishops to the last of the lay faithful', they show universal agreement in matters of faith and morals."[5] So the Bishop is called to lead his flock by "walking in front of them, showing them the way, showing them the path; walking in their midst, to strengthen them in unity; walking behind them, to make sure no one gets left behind but especially, never to lose the scent of the People of God in order to find new roads. A Bishop who lives among his faithful has his ears open to listen to 'what the Spirit says to the churches' (*Rev* 2:7), and to the 'voice of the sheep', also through those diocesan institutions whose task it is to advise the Bishop, promoting a loyal and constructive dialogue."[6]

Similarly, the Synod of Bishops must increasingly become a privileged instrument for *listening* to the People of God: "For the Synod Fathers we ask the Holy Spirit first of all for the gift of listening: to listen to God, that with him we may hear the cry of the people; to listen to the people until breathing in the desire to which God calls us."[7]

Although structurally it is essentially configured as an episcopal body, this does not mean that the Synod exists separately from the rest of the faithful. On the contrary, it is a suitable instrument to

---

[4]Apostolic Exhortation *Evangelii Gaudium*, 119.

[5]*Lumen Gentium*, 12.

[6]Address to the Participants in the Symposium for New Bishops promoted by the Congregation for Bishops and by the Congregation for Eastern Churches (19 September 2013). Cf. *Evangelii Gaudium*, 31.

[7]Address at the Vigil of Prayer in preparation for the Synod on the Family (4 October 2014).

give voice to the entire People of God, specifically via the Bishops, established by God as "authentic guardians, interpreters and witnesses of the faith of the whole Church,"[8] demonstrating, from one Assembly to another, that it is an eloquent expression of synodality as a "constitutive element of the Church."[9]

Therefore, as John Paul II declared, "Every General Assembly of the Synod of Bishops is a powerful ecclesial experience, even if some of its practical procedures can always be perfected. The Bishops assembled in Synod represent in the first place their own Churches, but they are also attentive to the contributions of the Episcopal Conferences which selected them and whose views about questions under discussion they then communicate. They thus express the recommendation of the entire hierarchical body of the Church and finally, in a certain sense, the whole Christian people, whose pastors they are."[10]

The history of the Church bears ample witness to the importance of consultation for ascertaining the views of the Bishops and the faithful in matters pertaining to the good of the Church. Hence, even in the preparation of Synodal Assemblies, it is very important that consultation of all the particular Churches be given special attention. In this initial phase, following the indications of the General Secretariat of the Synod, the Bishops submit the questions to be explored in the Synodal Assembly to the priests, deacons and lay faithful of their Churches, both individually and in associations, without overlooking the valuable contribution that consecrated men and women can offer. Above all, the contribution of the local Church's participatory bodies, especially the Presbyteral Council and the Pastoral Council, can prove fundamental, and from here "a synodal Church can begin to emerge."[11]

During every Synodal Assembly, consultation of the faithful

---

[8]Address on the Fiftieth Anniversary of the Synod of Bishops (17 October 2015).
[9]*Ibid.*
[10]Post-Synodal Apostolic Exhortation *Pastores Gregis*, 58.
[11]Address on the Fiftieth Anniversary of the Synod of Bishops. Cf. *Evangelii Gaudium*, 31.

must be followed by discernment on the part of the Bishops chosen for the task, united in the search for a consensus that springs not from worldly logic, but from common obedience to the Spirit of Christ. Attentive to the *sensus fidei* of the People of God—"which they need to distinguish carefully from the changing currents of public opinion"[12]—the members of the Assembly offer their opinion to the Roman Pontiff so that it can help him in his ministry as universal Pastor of the Church. From this perspective, "the fact that the Synod ordinarily has only a consultative role does not diminish its importance. In the Church the purpose of any collegial body, whether consultative or deliberative, is always the search for truth or the good of the Church. When it is therefore a question involving the faith itself, the *consensus ecclesiae* is not determined by the tallying of votes, but is the outcome of the working of the Spirit, the soul of the one Church of Christ."[13] Therefore the vote of the Synod Fathers, "if morally unanimous, has a qualitative ecclesial weight which surpasses the merely formal aspect of the consultative vote."[14]

Finally, the Synod Assembly itself must be followed by the implementation phase, so as to initiate the reception of the Synod's conclusions in all the local Churches, once they have been accepted by the Roman Pontiff in the manner he judges most appropriate. Here it must be remembered that "cultures are in fact quite diverse, and every general principle . . . needs to be inculturated, if it is to be respected and applied."[15] In this way, it can be seen that the synodal process not only has its point of departure but also its point of arrival in the People of God, upon whom the gifts of grace bestowed by the Holy Spirit through the gathering of Bishops in Assembly must be poured out.

The Synod of Bishops, which is "in some manner the image"

---

[12]Address on the Fiftieth Anniversary of the Synod of Bishops.

[13]Post-Synodal Apostolic Exhortation *Pastores Gregis*, 58.

[14]John Paul II, Address to the Council of the General Secretariat of the Synod of Bishops (30 April 1983).

[15]Closing Address of the XIV Ordinary General Assembly of the Synod of Bishops (24 October 2015).

of an Ecumenical Council and reflects its "spirit and method,"[16] is composed of Bishops. Nevertheless, as also happened at the Council,[17] certain others who are not Bishops may be summoned to the Synod Assembly; their role is determined in each case by the Roman Pontiff. In this connection, special consideration must be given to the contribution that can be offered by members of Institutes of Consecrated Life and Societies of Apostolic Life.

Besides the members, certain invited guests without voting rights may attend the Synod Assembly. These include Experts (*Periti*), who help with the redaction of documents; Auditors (*Auditores*), who have particular competence regarding the issues under discussion; Fraternal Delegates from Churches and Ecclesial Communities not yet in full communion with the Catholic Church. To these may be added further special guests (*Invitati Speciales*), chosen because of their acknowledged authority.

The Synod of Bishops meets in various types of gathering.[18] If circumstances so suggest, a single Synodal Assembly may be spread over more than one session. Each Assembly, whatever its format, is an important opportunity for collective listening to what the Holy Spirit "is saying to the churches" (*Rev* 2:7). In the course of the synodal deliberations, then, particular importance should be attached to liturgical celebrations and other forms of common prayer, so as to invoke the gifts of discernment and harmony upon the members of the assembly. It is also right and just, following an ancient synodal tradition, that the Book of the Gospels be solemnly enthroned at the start of each day, symbolically reminding all the participants of the need for docility to the divine word, which is the "word of truth" (*Col* 1:5).

---

[16]Paul VI, Address for the start of the sessions of the I Ordinary General Assembly of the Synod of Bishops (30 September 1967).

[17]Cf. *Codex Iuris Canonici*, can. 339, §2; *Codex Canonum Ecclesiarum Orientalium*, can. 52, §2.

[18]Cf. *Codex Iuris Canonici*, can. 346

Ecclesial Exercise in Discernment

Address at the Opening of the Synod of Bishops on Young People, the Faith and Vocational Discernment

OCTOBER 3, 2018

Dear Beatitudes, Eminences, Excellencies,
Dear Brothers and Sisters, and Beloved Young People!

Entering this hall to talk about young people, we already feel the strength of their presence that emanates a positivity and enthusiasm capable of filling and gladdening not only this hall, but the whole Church and the whole world.

That is why I cannot begin without saying thank you! I thank you who are present, I thank the many people, who throughout this two-year period of preparation have worked with dedication and passion—here in the Church of Rome and in all the Churches of the world—to enable us to reach this moment . . .

I would also like to sincerely thank the young people connected to us now, and all the youth who in so many ways have made their voices heard. I thank them for having wagered that it is worth the effort to feel part of the Church or to enter into dialogue with her; worth the effort to have the Church as a mother, as a teacher, as a home, as a family, and, despite human weaknesses and difficulties, capable of radiating and conveying Christ's timeless message; worth the effort to hold onto the boat of the Church which, despite the world's cruel storms, continues to offer shelter and hospitality to everyone; worth the effort to listen to one another; worth the effort to swim against the tide and be bound by lofty values: family, fidelity, love, faith, sacrifice, service, eternal life. Our responsibility here at the Synod is not to undermine them; but rather to show that they are right to wager: it truly is worth the effort, it is not a waste of time!

And I thank you in particular, dear young people present! The path of preparation for the Synod has taught us that the universe of the young is so varied that it cannot be fully represented, but you are certainly an important sign of it. Your participation fills us with joy and hope.

The Synod we are living is a moment of sharing. I wish, therefore, at the beginning of the Synod Assembly, to invite everyone to speak with courage and frankness *(parrhesia)*, namely to integrate *freedom, truth and charity*. Only dialogue can help us grow. An honest, transparent critique is constructive and helpful, and does not engage in useless chatter, rumors, conjectures or prejudices.

And humility in listening must correspond to courage in speaking. I told the young people in the pre-Synod Meeting: "If you say something I do not like, I have to listen even more, because everyone has the right to be heard, just as everyone has the right to speak." This open listening requires courage in speaking and in becoming the voice of many young people in the world who are not present. It is this listening that creates space for dialogue.

The Synod must be an exercise in dialogue, above all among those of you participating. The first fruit of this dialogue is that everyone is open to newness, to change their opinions thanks to what they have heard from others. This is important for the Synod. Many of you have already prepared your intervention beforehand—and I thank you for this work—but I invite you to feel free to consider what you have prepared as a provisional draft open to any additions and changes that the Synod journey may suggest to each of you. Let us feel free to welcome and understand others and therefore to change our convictions and positions: this is a sign of great human and spiritual maturity.

The Synod is an ecclesial exercise in discernment. To speak frankly and listen openly are fundamental if the Synod is to be a process of discernment. Discernment is not an advertising slogan, it is not an organizational technique, or a fad of this pontificate, but an *interior attitude* rooted in *an act of faith*. Discernment is the method and at the same time the goal we set ourselves: it is based on the conviction that God is at work in world history, in life's events, in the people I meet and who speak to me. For this reason, we are called to listen to what the Spirit suggests to us, with methods and in paths that are often unpredictable. Discernment needs space and time. And so, during the work done in plenary assembly and in groups, after five interventions are made, a moment of silence of approximately three minutes will be observed. This is to allow everyone to recognize within their hearts the nuances of what they have heard, and to allow everyone to reflect deeply and seize upon what is most striking. This attention to interiority is the key to accomplishing the work of recognizing, interpreting and choosing.

We are a sign of a Church that listens and journeys. The attitude of listening cannot be limited to the words we will exchange during the work of the Synod. The path of preparation for this moment has highlighted a Church that *needs to listen*, including those young people who often do not feel understood by the Church in their originality and therefore not accepted for who they really are, and sometimes even rejected. This Synod has the opportunity, the task and the duty to be a sign of a Church that really listens, that allows herself to be questioned by the experiences of those she meets, and who does not always have a ready-made answer. A Church that does not listen shows herself closed to newness, closed to God's surprises, and cannot be credible, especially for the young who will inevitably turn away rather than approach.

Let us leave behind prejudice and stereotypes. A first step towards listening is to free our minds and our hearts from prejudice and stereotypes. When we think we already know who others are and what they want, we really struggle to listen to them seriously. Relations across generations are a terrain in which prejudice and stereotypes take root with proverbial ease, so much so that we are often oblivious to it. Young people are tempted to consider adults outdated; adults are tempted to regard young people as inexperienced, to know how they are and especially how they should be and behave. All of this can be an overwhelming obstacle to dialogue and to the encounter between generations. Most of those present do not belong to a younger generation, so it is clear that we must pay attention, above all, to the risk of talking about young people in categories and ways of thinking that are already outmoded. If we can avoid this risk, then we will help to bridge generations. Adults should overcome the temptation to underestimate the abilities of young people and not judge them negatively.

I once read that the first mention of this fact dates back to 3000 BC and was discovered on a clay pot in ancient Babylon, where it is written that young people are immoral and incapable of saving their people's culture. This is an old tradition of us old ones! Young people, on the other hand, should overcome the temptation to ignore adults and to consider the elderly "archaic, outdated and boring," forgetting that it is foolish always to start from scratch as if life began only with each of them. Despite their physical frailty, the elderly are always the memory of mankind, the roots of our society, the "pulse" of our civilization. To spurn them, reject them, isolate or snub them is to yield to a worldly mentality that is devouring our homes from within. To neglect the rich experiences that each generation inherits and transmits to the next is an act of self-destruction.

It is therefore necessary, on the one hand, to decisively overcome the scourge of clericalism. Listening and leaving aside stereotypes are powerful antidotes to the risk of clericalism, to which an assembly such as this is inevitably exposed, despite our intentions. Clericalism arises from an elitist and exclusivist vision of vocation that interprets the ministry received as a *power* to be exercised rather than as a free and generous *service* to be given. This leads us to believe that we belong to a group that has all the answers and no longer needs to listen or learn anything, or that pretends to listen. *Clericalism is a perversion and is the root of many evils in the Church*: we must humbly ask forgiveness for this and above all create the conditions so that it is not repeated.

We must, on the other hand, cure the virus of self-sufficiency and of hasty conclusions reached by many young people. An Egyptian proverb goes: "If there is no elderly person in your home, buy one, because you will need him." To shun and reject everything handed down across the ages brings only a dangerous disorientation that sadly threatens our humanity, it brings a disillusionment which has invaded the hearts of whole generations. The accumulation of human experiences throughout history is the most precious and trustworthy treasure that one generation inherits from another. Without ever forgetting divine revelation, that enlightens and gives meaning to history and to our existence.

Brothers and sisters, may the Synod awaken our hearts! The present moment, and this applies also to the Church, appears to be laden with struggles, problems, burdens. But our faith tells us that it is also the *kairos* in which the Lord comes to meet us in order to love us and call us to the fullness of life. The future is not a threat to be feared, but is the time the Lord promises us when we will be able to experience communion with him, with our brothers and sisters, and with the whole of creation. We need to rediscover the reasons for our hope and, above all, to pass them on to young people who are thirsting for hope. As the Second Vatican Council affirmed: "We can justly consider that the future of humanity lies in the hands of those who are strong enough to provide coming generations with reasons for living and hoping" (Pastoral Constitution *Gaudium et Spes*, 31).

The meeting between generations can be extremely fruitful for giving rise to hope. The prophet Joel teaches us this—I reminded young people at the pre-Synod meeting—and I consider it *the prophecy of our time*: "Your old men shall dream dreams, and your young men shall see visions" (2:28) and they will prophesy.

There is no need for sophisticated theological arguments to prove our duty to help the contemporary world to walk towards God's kingdom, free of false hope and without seeing only ruin and woe. Indeed, when speaking about those who consider reality without sufficient objectivity or prudent judgment, Saint John XXIII said: "In the current conditions of human society they are not capable of seeing anything except ruin and woe; they go around saying that in our times, compared to the past, everything is worse; and they even go as far as to behave as if they had nothing to learn from history, which is our teacher" (*Address on the solemn opening of the Second Vatican Council*, 11 October 1962).

Do not let yourselves be tempted, therefore, by the "prophets of doom," do not spend your energy on "keeping score of failures and holding on to reproaches," keep your gaze fixed on the good that "often makes no sound; it is neither a topic for blogs, nor front page news," and do not be afraid "before the wounds of Christ's flesh, always inflicted by sin and often by the children of the Church" (cf. *Address to Bishops participating in the course promoted by the Congregation for Bishops and the Congregation for Oriental Churches*, 13 September 2018).

Let us therefore work to "spend time with the future," to take from this Synod not merely a document—that generally is only read by a few and criticized by many—but above all concrete pastoral proposals capable of fulfilling the Synod's purpose. In other words, *to plant dreams, draw forth prophecies and visions, allow hope to flourish, inspire trust, bind up wounds, weave together relationships, awaken a dawn of hope, learn from one another, and create a bright resourcefulness* that will enlighten minds, warm hearts, give strength to our hands, and inspire in young people—all young people, with no one excluded—a vision of the future filled with the joy of the Gospel. Thank you.

A Way of Being and Working Together

Angelus

Saint Peter's Square, October 28, 2018

A *synodal style* that does not have as its primary purpose the writing of a document, which is also valuable and useful. More than the document, however, it is important to promote a way of being and working together, young and old, in listening and in discernment, in order to arrive at pastoral choices that respond to reality.

Youth Ministry Is Always Synodal

Apostolic Exhortation, Christus Vivit *(nns. 202–208)*
To Young People and to the Entire People of God

March 25, 2019

Youth ministry, as traditionally carried out, has been significantly affected by social and cultural changes. Young people frequently fail to find in our usual programs a response to their concerns, their needs, their problems and issues. The proliferation and growth of groups and movements predominantly associated with the young can be considered the work of the Holy Spirit who constantly shows us new paths. Even so, there is a need to look at the ways such groups participate in the Church's overall pastoral care, as well as a need for greater communion among them and a better coordination of their activities. Although it is never easy to approach young people, two things have become increasingly evident: the realization that the entire community has to be involved in evangelizing them, and the urgent requirement that young people take on a greater role in pastoral outreach.

A pastoral care that is synodal

I want to state clearly that young people themselves are agents of youth ministry. Certainly they need to he helped and guided, but at the same time left free to develop new approaches, with creativity and a certain audacity. So I will not attempt here to propose a kind of manual of youth ministry or a practical pastoral guide. I am more concerned with helping young people to use their insight, ingenuity and knowledge to address the issues and concerns of other young people in their own language.

The young make us see the need for new styles and new strategies. For example, while adults often worry about having everything properly planned, with regular meetings and fixed times, most young people today have little interest in this kind of pastoral approach. Youth ministry needs to become more flexible: inviting young people to events or occasions that provide an opportunity not only for learning, but also for conversing, celebrating, singing, listening to real stories and experiencing a shared encounter with the living God.

At the same time, we should take into greater consideration those practices that have shown their value—the methods, language and aims that have proved truly effective in bringing young people to Christ and the Church. It does not matter where they are coming from or what labels they have received, whether "conservative" or "liberal," "traditional" or "progressive." What is important is that we make use of everything that has borne good fruit and effectively communicates the joy of the Gospel.

Youth ministry has to be synodal; it should involve a "journeying together" that values "the charisms that the Spirit bestows in accordance with the vocation and role of each of the Church's members, through a process of co-responsibility . . . Motivated by this spirit, we can move towards a participatory and co-responsible Church, one capable of appreciating its own rich variety, gratefully accepting the contributions of the lay faithful, including young people and women, consecrated persons, as well as groups, associations and movements. No one should be excluded or exclude themselves." (*Final Document of the Fifteenth Ordinary General Assembly of the Synod of Bishops*, 123)

In this way, by learning from one another, we can better reflect that wonderful multifaceted reality that Christ's Church is meant to be. She will be able to attract young people, for her unity is not monolithic, but rather a network of varied gifts that the Spirit ceaselessly pours out upon her, renewing her and lifting her up from her poverty.

In the Synod, many concrete proposals emerged for renewing

youth ministry and freeing it from approaches that are no longer effective because they are incapable of entering into dialogue with contemporary youth culture. Naturally, I cannot list them all here. A number of them can be found in the Final Document of the Synod.

What the Lord Asks of Us Is Already Contained in the Word Synod

From Address to the General Assembly of the Italian Bishops Conference

May 20, 2019

Dear Brothers,

I thank you for this meeting, which I would like to be a moment of help in pastoral discernment on the life and mission of the Italian Church. I also thank you for the effort you offer every day in carrying out the mission the Lord has entrusted to you and in serving the people of God with and according to the heart of the Good Shepherd. . . .

On the occasion of the commemoration of the 50th anniversary of the establishment of the Synod of Bishops, held on October 17, 2015, I wanted to clarify that "the path of synodality is the path that God expects from the Church of the third millennium [. . .] it is a constitutive dimension of the Church," so that "what the Lord asks of us, in a sense, is already all contained in the word synod."[1]

Also the new document of the International Theological Commission, on synodality in the life and mission of the Church, at its 2017 Plenary Session, states that "synodality, in the ecclesiological context, indicates the specific *modus vivendi et operandi* of the Church People of God that manifests and realizes in concrete terms its being in communion in walking together, gathering in assembly, and in the active participation of all its members in its

[1]AAS 107 (2015), 1139.

evangelizing mission." It goes on to say, "While the concept of *synodality* recalls the involvement and participation of the whole People of God in the life and mission of the Church, the concept of *collegiality* specifies the theological meaning and form of the exercise of the ministry of the bishops at the service of the particular Church entrusted to the pastoral care of each one and in communion among the particular Churches within the one and universal Church of Christ, through the hierarchical communion of the College of Bishops with the Bishop of Rome. Collegiality, therefore, is the specific form in which ecclesial synodality is manifested and realized through the ministry of the bishops on the level of communion among the particular Churches in a region and on the level of communion among all the Churches in the universal Church. Every authentic manifestation of synodality by its very nature requires the exercise of the collegial ministry of the bishops."[2]

Therefore, I rejoice that this assembly wanted to explore this topic, which actually describes the *medical record* of the health of the Italian Church and your pastoral and ecclesiastical work. . . .

On synodality, even in the context of a probable Synod for the Italian Church, I heard a "noise" lately about this, it went all the way to Santa Marta! There are two directions: *synodality from the bottom up*, that is, having to take care of the existence and good functioning of the diocese—the councils, the parishes, the involvement of the laity . . . (cf. *CIC* 469–494)—starting with the dioceses: you cannot have a great synod without going to the base. This is the movement from the bottom up—and the evaluation of the role of the laity. And then there is *synodality from the top down*, in accordance with the speech I addressed to the Italian Church at the Fifth National Convention in Florence, November 10, 2015, which still remains in force and must accompany us on this journey. If someone is thinking of having a synod on the Italian Church, it has to start both from the bottom up, and from the top down. And that will take time, but you will walk on solid ground, not on ideas.

---

[2]http://www.vatican.va/roman_curia/congregations/cfaith/cti_documents/rc_cti_20180302_sinodalita_it.html.

A Journey under the Guidance of the Holy Spirit

Letter to the Pilgrim People of God in Germany

JUNE 29, 2019

Dear Brothers and Sisters,

The contemplation of the readings of the Easter feast from the Acts of the Apostles has moved me to write this letter to you. In these readings we meet the very first apostolic community, completely imbued with the new life given by the Holy Spirit who, at the same time, arranged all the circumstances in such a way that they became good occasions for proclamation. The disciples at that time seemed to have lost everything and on the first day of the week, between bitterness and sadness, they heard from the mouth of a woman that the Lord was alive. Nothing and no one could stop the penetration of the Paschal Mystery into their lives and at the same time the disciples could not comprehend what their eyes had seen and their hands had touched (cf. 1 Jn 1:1).

In view of this, and with the conviction that the Lord "with his newness can always renew our life and our community,"[1] I would like to be close to you and share your concern for the future of the Church in Germany. We are all aware that we are not only living in a time of change, but rather in a turning point in time, which raises new and old questions, in view of which a debate is justified and necessary. The situations and questions that I was able to discuss with your pastors on the occasion of the last *ad limina*

[1]Francis, Apostolic Exhortation *Evangelii Gaudium*, 11.

visit certainly continue to resonate in your communities. As on that occasion, I would like to offer you my support, to express my closeness to you on the common journey, and to encourage you to search for a frank response to the present situation.

1. With gratitude I contemplate the fine network of congregations and communities, parishes and daughter parishes, schools and colleges, hospitals and other social institutions that have come into being throughout history and bear witness to a living faith that has sustained, nurtured and animated them over several generations. This faith has passed through times determined by suffering, confrontation and tribulation, and at the same time is characterized by permanence and vitality; even today it shows itself rich in fruit in many testimonies of life and in works of charity. The Catholic communities in Germany, in their diversity and plurality, are recognized worldwide for their sense of co-responsibility and generosity, which has known how to reach out and accompany the implementation of evangelization processes in regions in disadvantaged areas that lack opportunities. This generosity has shown itself in recent history not only in the form of economic and material aid, but also by sharing numerous charisms and sending out personnel over the years: priests, religious women and men, and lay people who have been completely faithful and tireless in fulfilling their ministry and mission in often very difficult conditions.[2] You have given to the universal Church great holy men and women, great theologians and spiritual shepherds and lay people, who have made their contribution to the success of a fruitful encounter between the Gospel and cultures, towards new syntheses and capable of awakening the best of both for future generations in the same zeal of the beginnings.[3] This has made possible remarkable efforts to find pastoral responses to the challenges you have faced.

I would also like to point out the ecumenical journey you

---

[2]Cf. Benedict XVI, Meeting with the German Bishops in Cologne, XX World Youth Day (August 21, 2005).

[3]Cf. Vatican Council II, Pastoral Constitution *Gaudium et Spes*, 58.

have embarked upon, the fruits of which were evident during the commemorative year of "500 years of the Reformation." This path encourages further initiatives in prayer as well as cultural exchanges and works of charity that enable us to overcome the prejudices and wounds of the past so that we can better celebrate and witness to the joy of the Gospel.

2. Today, however, I painfully note with you the increasing erosion and decay of the faith, with all that this implies not only on the spiritual level, but also on the social and cultural levels. This situation can be visibly noted, as Benedict XVI has already pointed out, not only "in the East, as we know, where a large part of the population is not baptized and has no contact with the Church and often does not know Christ at all,"[4] but even in so-called "traditionally Catholic areas with a drastic decrease in attendance at Sunday Mass as well as in the reception of the sacraments."[5] This is certainly a multi-faceted decline, and one that is neither soon nor easily solvable. It demands a serious and conscious approach and challenges us in this historical moment like that beggar, when we too hear the Apostle's word: "Silver and gold I do not possess. But what I have, I give to you: In the name of Jesus Christ the Nazarene, arise and walk!" (Acts 3:6)

3. To face this situation, your bishops have proposed a synodal way. What this means in concrete terms and how it develops will certainly have to be considered in greater depth. For my part, I have presented my reflections on synodality on the occasion of the celebration of the 50th anniversary of the Synod of Bishops.[6] It is, in essence, a *synodos*, a common journey under the guidance of the Holy Spirit. But this means setting out together on the journey with the whole Church under the light of the Holy Spirit, under his guidance and stirring, in order to learn to listen and to recog-

---

[4]Benedict XVI, Meeting with the German Bishops in Cologne, XX World Youth Day (August 21, 2005).

[5]Francis, *Ad limina* Visit of the German Bishops (Nov. 20, 2015).

[6]Cf. Francis, Apostolic Constitution *Episcopalis Communio* (Sept. 15, 2018).

nize the ever new horizon that he wants to give us. For synodality presupposes and needs the action of the Holy Spirit.

On the occasion of the last Plenary Assembly of the Italian Bishops, I had the opportunity to recall once again this reality, central to the life of the Church, by introducing the double perspective that it follows: "Synodality from the bottom up means the duty to take care of the existence and proper functioning of the diocese, of the councils, of the parishes, of the participation of the laity . . . (cf. cann. 469–494 CIC), beginning with the diocese. Thus, it is not possible to hold a great synod without considering the grassroots . . ." Only then does synodality come "from the top down," which allows us to live in a specific and particular way the collegial dimension of episcopal ministry and of being Church.[7] Only in this way will we arrive at mature decisions in matters essential to the faith and life of the Church. This will be possible on condition that we set out on the journey, equipped with patience and the humble and healthy conviction that we will never succeed in solving all the questions and problems at once. The Church is and will always be a pilgrim on the path of history, carrying a treasure in earthen vessels (cf. 2 Cor 4:7). This reminds us: in this world the Church will never be perfect, while her vitality and her beauty are founded in that treasure which she was appointed to guard from the beginning.[8]

The current challenges, as well as the responses we give, in view of the development of a healthy *aggiornamento,* require "a long process of maturation and the collaboration of a whole people

---

[7]Cf. Vatican Council II, Dogmatic Constitution on the Church *Lumen Gentium*, 23; Council Decree on the Ministry of Bishops *Christus Dominus*, 3. Quoting the *International Theological Commission* from its recent document, *Synodality in the Life and Mission of the Church*, I told the Italian bishops: "Collegiality, therefore, is the specific form in which ecclesial synodality is expressed; it is realized through the ministry of bishops at the level of *communion* among the particular Churches of a region and through *communion* among all the particular Churches in the universal Church. Any authentic expression of synodality requires, by its very nature, the collegial ministry of the bishops." Cf. Address to the Italian Bishops' Conference (May 20, 2019).

[8]Cf. Vatican Council II, Dogmatic Constitution on the Church *Lumen Gentium*, 8.

over years."[9] This stimulates the emergence and continuation of processes that build us up as the people of God, instead of looking for immediate results with hasty and medial consequences that are fleeting because of a lack of deepening and maturation or because they do not correspond to the vocation we have been given.

4. In this sense, with all the serious and unavoidable reflection, it is easy to fall into subtle temptations to which, in my opinion, we should pay special attention and therefore exercise caution, since, anything but helpful for a common path, they keep us stuck in preconceived schemes and mechanisms that end in alienation or a limitation of our mission. Even more, as an aggravating circumstance, if we are not aware of these temptations, we easily end up in a complicated series of arguments, analyses, and solutions with no other effect than to keep us away from the real and daily encounter with the faithful people and the Lord.

5. Accepting and bearing the present situation does not imply passivity or resignation, and even less negligence; on the contrary, it is an invitation to face what has died in us and in our communities, what needs evangelization and the Lord's visitation. But this requires courage, because what we need is much more than a structural, organizational, or functional change.

I recall what I said on the occasion of the meeting with your pastors in 2015, namely that one of the first and greatest temptations in the ecclesial field is to believe that the solutions to current and future problems can be achieved exclusively through the reform of structures, organizations, and administration, but that in the end these do not touch in any way the vital points that really need attention. "It is a kind of new Pelagianism that leads us to put our trust in administration, in the perfect apparatus. But excessive centralization complicates the life of the Church and her missionary dynamism, instead of helping her (cf. *Evangelii Gaudium*, 32)."[10]

The basis of this temptation is the idea that the best response

---

[9]Yves Congar, *True and False Reform in the Church.*

[10]Francis, Address to the German Bishops' Conference (Nov. 20, 2015).

to the many problems and shortcomings is to reorganize things, to make changes and to "patch things up" in order to order and smooth out ecclesiastical life, adapting it to the current logic or that of a particular group. In such a way, all the difficulties seem to be solved and things seem to find their way again, so that the ecclesial life finds a "certain" new or old order, which then puts an end to the tensions that are proper to our being human and that the Gospel wants to evoke.[11]

In this way, tensions in church life would only seem to be eliminated. To want only to be "in order and in harmony" would in time only put to sleep and tame the heart of our people and reduce or even silence the living power of the Gospel that the Spirit wants to give: "But this would be the greatest sin of secularization and worldly mindedness against the Gospel."[12] In this way, we would perhaps arrive at a well-structured and functioning, even "modernized" ecclesial organism; however, it would remain without soul and without the freshness of the Gospel. We would merely live a "gaseous," vague Christianity, but without the necessary "bite" of the Gospel.[13] "Today we are called to face imbalances and disproportions. We will not be able to do anything good according to the Gospel if we are afraid of it."[14] We must not forget that there are tensions and imbalances that have the flavor of the Gospel, that are to be maintained because they promise new life.

6. Therefore, it seems to me important not to lose sight of what "the Church has repeatedly taught, that we are not justified by our

---

[11]Ultimately, it is the logic of a technocratic thinking that imposes itself on all the decisions, relationships and nuances of our lives (cf. Francis, Encyclical *Laudato si'*, 106–114). Therefore, such logic also influences our thinking and feeling and our way of loving God and neighbor.

[12]Francis, Diocesan Assembly of the Diocese of Rome (May 9, 2019).

[13]Cf. Francis, Apostolic Exhortation *Evangelii Gaudium*, 97: "God save us from a worldly Church with superficial spiritual and pastoral trappings! This stifling worldliness can only be healed by breathing in the pure air of the Holy Spirit who frees us from self-centeredness cloaked in an outward religiosity bereft of God. Let us not allow ourselves to be robbed of the Gospel!"

[14]Francis, Diocesan Assembly of the Diocese of Rome (May 9, 2019).

works or our efforts, but by the grace of the Lord who takes the initiative."[15] Without this dimension of divine virtues, we run the risk of repeating in the various renewal efforts what today prevents the ecclesial community from proclaiming the merciful love of God. The way in which we accept the present situation will determine the fruits that will develop from it. Therefore, I appeal that this be done in the tone of divine virtues. Let the Gospel of grace with the visitation of the Holy Spirit be the light and guide for you to face these challenges. As often as an ecclesiastical community has tried to get out of its problems alone, relying only on its own powers, methods, and intelligence, it has ended up multiplying and perpetuating the evils it wanted to overcome. Forgiveness and salvation are not something that we have to buy, "or that we have to acquire by our works or our efforts. He forgives and frees us gratuitously. His giving of Himself on the cross is something so great that we cannot and should not pay for it; we can only receive this gift with the greatest gratitude, full of joy at being so loved before we even think of it."[16]

The current situation does not allow us to lose sight of the fact that our mission is not based on forecasts, calculations, or encouraging or discouraging surveys, neither at the ecclesial, political, economic or social level, nor on the successful results of our pastoral planning.[17] All this is important to evaluate, to listen, to evaluate, and to pay attention to these things, but in itself it does not exhaust our being believers. Our mission and reason for being is rooted in the fact that "God so loved the world that he gave his only Son, that whoever believes in him should not perish but have eternal life" (Jn 3:16). "Without new life and genuine spirit inspired by

---

[15]Francis, Apostolic Exhortation *Gaudete et Exsultate*, 52.

[16]Francis, Night Synodal Apostolic Exhortation *Christus Vivit*, 121.

[17]An attitude that either kindles a spirit of unrestrained desire for success in the case of a favorable wind or produces a sacrificial attitude when "it is necessary to row against the wind." These ways of thinking are alien to the spirit of the Gospel, and allow an elitist practice of faith to shine through. Neither the one, nor the other; the Christian lives by thanksgiving.

the Gospel, without 'fidelity of the Church to her own vocation,' any new structure will perish in a short time."[18]

Therefore, the upcoming process of change cannot respond exclusively in a reactive way to external facts and necessities, such as the sharp decline in the number of births and the aging of the congregations, which do not allow to envisage a normal generational change. However, objective and valid causes, if considered in isolation from the mystery of the Church, would favor and stimulate a merely reactive attitude, both positive and negative. A true process of transformation responds, but at the same time makes demands that spring from our being Christians and from the intrinsic dynamism of the Church's evangelization; such a process demands a pastoral conversion. We are asked to adopt an attitude aimed at living the Gospel and making it transparent, breaking with "the gray pragmatism of the daily life of the Church, in which all appears to proceed normally, while in reality faith is wearing down and degenerating into small-mindedness."[19] Pastoral conversion reminds us that evangelization must be our guiding criterion par excellence, under which we can discern all the steps we are called to set in motion as an ecclesial community; evangelization constitutes the proper and essential mission of the Church.[20]

7. Therefore, as your Bishops have already stressed, it is necessary to regain the primacy of evangelization in order to face the future with confidence and hope, because "the Church, bearer of evangelization, begins by evangelizing herself. As a community of believers, as a community of lived and preached hope, as a community of fraternal love, the Church herself must ceaselessly hear what she must believe, what are the reasons for her hope, and what is the new commandment of love."[21]

Evangelization lived in this way is not a tactic of ecclesial re-

---

[18]Francis, Apostolic Exhortation *Evangelii Gaudium*, 26.
[19]Francis, Apostolic Exhortation *Evangelii Gaudium*, 83.
[20]Cf. Paul VI, Apostolic Exhortation *Evangelii Nuntiandi*, 14.
[21]Ibid., 15.

positioning in today's world, or an act of conquest, domination, or territorial expansion; it is not a "retouching" that adapts the Church to the spirit of the times but makes her lose her originality and prophetic mission. Nor does evangelization mean an attempt to recover habits and practices that made sense in other cultural contexts. No, evangelization is a path of discipleship in response to love for the One who first loved us (cf. 1 Jn 4:19); a path, then, that makes possible a faith that is lived, experienced, celebrated, and witnessed with joy. Evangelization leads us to recover the joy of the Gospel, the joy of being Christians.

There are certainly hard moments and times of the cross, but nothing can destroy the supernatural joy that knows how to adapt, to change, and that always remains, like a light, even if slight, that comes from the personal certainty of being infinitely loved, beyond everything else. Evangelization produces inner security, "a serene hope and a spiritual fulfilment that the world cannot understand or appreciate."[22] Disgruntlement, apathy, bitterness, craving for criticism, as well as sadness are not good signs or counselors; rather, there are times when "sadness can be a sign of ingratitude. We can get so caught up in ourselves that we are unable to recognize God's gifts."[23]

8. Therefore, our main focus must be how we communicate this joy: by opening ourselves and going out to meet our brothers and sisters, especially those who are found at the thresholds of our church doors, on the streets, in the prisons, in the hospitals, in the squares and in the cities. The Lord expressed himself clearly: "But seek first his kingdom and his righteousness; then all the rest will be added to you" (Mt 6:33). This means going out to anoint with the Spirit of Christ all the realities of this earth, at its many crossroads, especially "where the new stories and paradigms are emerging, to reach with the Word of Jesus the innermost core of

---

[22]Cf. Francis, Apostolic Exhortation *Gaudete et Exsultate*, 125.

[23]Ibid., 126.

the soul of our cities."[24] This means helping so that the passion of Christ can truly and concretely touch that manifold suffering and those situations where his face continues to suffer from sin and inequality. May this suffering tear off the mask of the old and new forms of slavery that hurt men and women alike, especially today as we face anew xenophobic speeches that promote a culture based on indifference, closed-mindedness, individualism and expulsion. And, in turn, let it be the suffering of Christ that awakens passion for His kingdom in our parishes and communities, especially among the younger people!

This requires us to "find a spiritual delight in being close to people's lives, to the point of discovering that this is a source of higher joy. Mission is a passion for Jesus, but at the same time a passion for his people."[25]

Thus we would have to ask ourselves what the Spirit is saying to the Church today (cf. Rev 2:7) in order to discern the signs of the times,[26] which is not the same as merely conforming to the spirit of the times (cf. Rom 12:2). All the efforts of listening, deliberating and discerning are aimed at making the Church daily more faithful, available, dexterous and transparent in proclaiming the joy of the Gospel, the foundation on which all questions can find light and answers.[27] "Challenges exist to be overcome! Let us be realists, but without losing our joy, our boldness and our hope-filled commitment. Let us not allow ourselves to be robbed of missionary vigor!"[28]

9. The Second Vatican Council was an important step in the formation of the Church's awareness both of herself and of her mission in today's world. This journey, which began more than fifty years ago, continues to spur us to its reception and further development and, in any case, has not yet reached its end, espe-

---

[24]Francis, Apostolic Exhortation *Evangelii Gaudium*, 74.
[25]Ibid., 268.
[26]Cf. Vatican Council II, Pastoral Constitution *Gaudium et Spes*, 4; 11.
[27]Cf. Francis, Apostolic Exhortation *Evangelii Gaudium*, 28.
[28]Ibid., 109.

cially with regard to synodality, which is called to unfold at the various levels of ecclesial life (parish, dioceses, at the national level, in the universal Church, and in the various congregations and communities). It is the task of this process, especially in these times of strong fragmentation and polarization, to ensure that the *Sensus Ecclesiae* actually lives in every decision we make, nourishing and permeating all levels. It is a matter of living and sensing with the Church and in the Church, which in not a few situations will also cause us suffering in the Church and to the Church. The universal Church lives in and from the particular Churches,[29] just as the particular Churches live and flourish in and from the universal Church; if they were separated from the universal Church, they would weaken, deteriorate, and die. Hence the need to keep communion with the whole body of the Church always alive and effective. This helps us to overcome the fear that isolates us in ourselves and in our particularities, so that we can look the person in the eye and listen, or so that we can renounce needs and thus be able to accompany the one who has been left by the roadside. Sometimes this attitude can show itself in a minimal gesture, like that of the father of the Prodigal Son, who holds the doors open so that the son, when he returns, can enter without difficulty.[30] This does not mean not going, not advancing, not changing anything, and perhaps not even debating and disagreeing, but it is simply the consequence of knowing that we are essentially part of a larger Body that claims us, waits for us, and needs us, and that we also claim, expect, and need. It is the joy of feeling part of the holy and patient faithful people of God.

The challenges ahead, the various themes and issues cannot be ignored or obscured; they must be faced, taking care that we do not become entangled in them and lose our vision, the horizon thereby limiting itself and reality crumbling. "But if we remain trapped in

[29]Cf. Vatican Council II, Dogmatic Constitution on the Church *Lumen Gentium*, 23.

[30]Cf. Francis, Apostolic Exhortation *Evangelii Gaudium*, 46.

conflict, we lose our sense of the profound unity of reality."[31] In this sense, the *Sensus Ecclesiae* gives us this wide horizon of possibility from which to try to respond to the urgent questions. The *Sensus Ecclesiae reminds* us at the same time of the beauty of the multiform face of the Church.[32] This face is diverse, not only from a spatial perspective, in her peoples, races and cultures,[33] but also from her temporal reality, which allows us to immerse ourselves in the sources of the most living and full tradition. For its part, this tradition is called to keep the fire alive, instead of merely preserving the ashes.[34] It allows all generations to rekindle the first love with the help of the Holy Spirit.

The *Sensus Ecclesiae* frees us from selfishness and ideological tendencies to give us a taste of this certainty of the Second Vatican Council when it affirmed that the anointing of the Holy One (cf. 1 Jn 2:20. 27) belongs to the totality of the faithful.[35] Communion with the holy and faithful people of God, the bearers of the anointing, keeps alive the hope and certainty that the Lord walks by our side and that it is He who sustains our steps. A healthy common being-on-the-way must allow this conviction to shine through in the search for mechanisms through which all voices, especially those of the simple and small, can find space and be heard. The anointing of the Holy One, poured out on the whole ecclesial body, "distributes special graces among the faithful of every state and condition of life, *distributing his gifts to each according to his will* (1 Cor 12:11). By these he makes them fit and ready to undertake various works and services for the renewal and full building up of the Church, according to the saying, *To each*

---

[31]Francis, Apostolic Exhortation *Evangelii Gaudium*, 226.

[32]Cf. John Paul II, Apostolic Letter *Novo Millennio Ineunte*, 40.

[33]Cf. Vatican Council II, Dogmatic Constitution on the Church *Lumen Gentium*, 13.

[34]Gustav Mahler (attributed): "Tradition is the guarantee of the future and not the keeper of the ashes."

[35]Cf. Vatican Council II, Dogmatic Constitution on the Church *Lumen Gentium*, 12.

is given the evidence of the Spirit for his use (1 Cor. 12:7)."[36] This helps us to pay attention to this ancient and always new temptation of the promoters of Gnosticism, who, in order to make their own name and increase the reputation of their doctrine and their fame, have tried to say something always new and different from what the Word of God has given them. It is what St. John describes with the term *proagon* (2 Jn 9); it means the one who wants to be ahead, the advanced one, the one who pretends to go beyond the "ecclesiastical we . . ."[37]

10. Therefore, be attentive to every temptation that leads to wanting to reduce the people of God to an enlightened group, not allowing to see, rejoice in and give thanks for the inconspicuous, scattered holiness. This holiness that lives "in the patience of God's people: those parents who raise their children with immense love, in those men and women who work hard to support their families, in the sick, in elderly religious who never lose their smile. In their daily perseverance I see the holiness of the Church militant. Very often it is a holiness found in our next-door neighbors, those who, living in our midst, reflect God's presence."[38] This is the holiness that protects and has always preserved the Church from any ideological, pseudo-scientific, and manipulative reduction. This holiness stimulates us, reminds us and invites us to develop this Marian style in the missionary activity of the Church, which is thus able to express justice with mercy, contemplation with action and tenderness with conviction. "Whenever we look to Mary, we come to believe once again in the revolutionary nature of love and tenderness. In her we see that humility and tenderness are not virtues of the weak but of the strong who need not treat others poorly in order to feel important themselves."

"Because every time we look at Mary, we believe again in the

---

[36]Cf. Vatican Council II, Dogmatic Constitution on the Church *Lumen Gentium*, 12.

[37]Cf. Joseph Ratzinger, *The God of Jesus Christ* (Munich, 1976), p. 142.

[38]Francis, Apostolic Exhortation *Gaudete et Exsultate*, 7.

revolutionary of tenderness and love. In her we see that humility and tenderness are not virtues of the weak, but of the strong, who do not need to treat others badly in order to feel important."[39]

In my homeland, there is a thought-provoking and powerful proverb that can shed light on this: "Let the brothers be united, for this is the first law: let them maintain unity at all times, for if they fight among themselves, they will be devoured by the outsiders."[40] Brothers and sisters, let us have concern for one another! Let us watch out for the temptation of the father of lies and division, the master of division, who in driving the search for an apparent good or an answer to a particular situation, ultimately dismembers the body of God's holy and faithful people! Let us set out together as apostolic bodies and listen to one another under the guidance of the Holy Spirit—even if we do not think in the same way—out of the wise conviction that "the Church, in the course of the centuries, is constantly striving towards the fullness of divine truth, until God's words are fulfilled in her."[41]

11. The synodal vision does not cancel out oppositions or confusions, nor does it subordinate conflicts to the decisions of a "good consensus" that compromise the faith, to the results of censuses or surveys that arise on this or that subject. That would be very limiting. With the background and centrality of evangelization and the *Sensus Ecclesiae* as defining elements of our ecclesial DNA, synodality consciously claims to adopt a way of being Church in which "the whole is greater than the part, but it is also greater than the sum of its parts. There is no need, then, to be overly obsessed with limited and particular questions. We constantly have to broaden our horizons and see the greater good which will benefit us all. But this has to be done without evasion or uprooting. We need to sink our roots deeper into the fertile soil and history of our native place, which is a gift of God. We can work on a small

---

[39]Francis, Apostolic Exhortation *Evangelii Gaudium*, 288.

[40]José Hernandez, Martín Fierro, secunda parte, *Decimoséptima Sextina*.

[41]Vatican Council II, Dogmatic Constitution on Divine Revelation *Dei Verbum*, 8.

scale, in our own neighborhood, but with a larger perspective."[42]

12. This requires of all God's people, and especially of their pastors, an attitude of vigilance and conversion that makes it possible to preserve the life and effectiveness of these realities. Vigilance and conversion are gifts that only the Lord can give us. It must be enough for us to ask for his grace through prayer and fasting. It has always impressed me how the Lord was tempted in a special way during his earthly life, especially in the moments of great decisions. Prayer and fasting had a special and determining significance for all his subsequent actions (cf. Mt 4:1–11). Synodality, too, cannot escape this logic and must always be accompanied by the grace of conversion, so that our personal and communal action may increasingly conform to and represent the *kenosis of* Christ (cf. Phil 2:1–11). Speaking, acting, and responding as the Body of Christ also means speaking and acting in the manner of Christ with the same attitudes, prudence and priorities. Following the example of the Master who "emptied himself and became like a slave" (Phil 2:7), the grace of conversion therefore frees us from false and sterile protagonisms. It frees us from the temptation to remain in protected and comfortable positions, and invites us to go to the edges to find ourselves and to listen better to the Lord.

This attitude of divestment also allows us to experience the creative and always abundant power of hope born of the Gospel poverty to which we are called; it frees us to evangelize and to witness. In this way, we allow the Spirit to refresh and renew our lives, freeing them from slavery, indolence, and secondary comforts that prevent us from going out and, above all, from worshipping. For in worship man fulfills his highest duty and it allows him to glimpse the coming clarity that helps us to taste the new creation.[43]

Without this perspective, we run the risk of starting from ourselves or from the desire for self-justification and self-preservation, which leads to changes and regulations that get stuck halfway. Far

[42]Francis, Apostolic Exhortation *Evangelii Gaudium*, 235.

[43]Cf. Romano Guardini, *Glaubenserkenntnis*, Mainz 3rd ed. 1997, p.16.

from solving the problems, we end up getting caught in an endless spiral, suffocating and killing the most beautiful, liberating and promising proclamation that we have and that gives meaning to our existence: Jesus Christ is Lord! We need the prayer, the penance and the adoration that allow us to say with the publican: "God, be merciful to me a sinner!" (Lk 18:13), not in a hypocritical, infantile or pusillanimous way, but with the courage to open the door and see what usually remains hidden by superficiality, by the culture of well-being and appearances.[44]

Basically, these attitudes—true spiritual remedies (prayer, penance, and adoration), allow us to experience once again that to be a Christian means to know oneself blessed and thus a bearer of blessing for others. To be a Christian means to belong to the Church of the Beatitudes for the blessed of today: the poor, the hungry, those who mourn, the despised, the excluded and the reviled (cf. Lk 6:20–23). Let us not forget: "In the Beatitudes the Lord shows us the way. If we follow the way of the Beatitudes, we can reach the truest human and divine happiness. The Beatitudes are the mirror that lets us know with a glance if we are walking on a right path: This mirror does not lie!"[45]

13. Dear brothers and sisters, I know of your steadfastness and I am aware of what you have endured and suffered for the name of the Lord; I also know of your desire and longing to revive the first love in the Church with the power of the Spirit (cf. Rev 2:1–5). May this Spirit, who does not break the broken reed or extinguish the smoldering wick (cf. Is 42:3), nourish and revive the good that characterizes your people and make it flourish! I want to stand by you and accompany you in the certainty that if the Lord deems us worthy of living this hour, He has not done so to shame or paralyze us in the face of challenges. Rather, He wants His Word to once again challenge and ignite our hearts, as He did for your

---

[44]Cf. J. M. Bergoglio, *Sobre la acusación de sí*, 2.

[45]Francis' address to the 5th National Congress of the Church in Italy, Florence, November 10, 2015.

fathers, so that your sons and daughters might receive visions and your elders might once again receive prophetic dreams (cf. Joel 3:1). His love "allows us to lift up our heads and begin anew. Let us not flee from the resurrection of Jesus, let us never admit defeat, whatever may happen. Nothing shall be stronger than his life that drives us forward!"[46]

And so I ask you, pray for me!

[46]Francis, Apostolic Exhortation *Evangelii Gaudium*, 3.

"Being" Synod, Not "Having" a Synod

Address to the Members of the Permanent Synod of the Greek-Catholic Church of Ukraine

July 5, 2019

Eminences, Excellencies, Dear Brothers!

It was my wish to invite you here to Rome for fraternal sharing, also with the superiors of the competent dicasteries of the Roman Curia. I thank you for accepting the invitation; it is good to see you. Ukraine has for some time been experiencing a difficult and delicate situation, for more than five years wounded by a conflict that many describe as "hybrid," composed as it is of acts of war in which those responsible camouflage themselves; a conflict where the weakest and the smallest pay the highest price; a conflict aggravated by propagandist falsifications and manipulations of various types, also in the attempt to involve the religious aspect.

I hold you in my heart and I pray for you, dear Ukrainian brothers. And I confide to you that at times I do so with prayers that I remember and that I learned from Bishop Stepan Czmil, then a Salesian priest; he taught me them when I was twelve years old, in 1949, and I learned from him to serve the Divine Liturgy three times a week. I thank you for your fidelity to the Lord and to Peter's Successor, which has often cost dearly throughout history, and I beg the Lord to accompany the actions of all those with political responsibility to search not the so-called partisan good, which in the end is always an interest at someone else's expense, but the common good, peace. And I ask of the "God of all comfort" (*2 Cor* 1: 3), to comfort the souls of those who have lost their loved ones due to the war, those who bear wounds in their body and in their spirit, those who have had to leave their home and work, and face the risk of searching a more human future elsewhere, far away. Know that my gaze goes every morning to the Madonna which His Beatitude gave to me, when he left Buenos Aires to assume the office of major Archbishop that the Church had entrusted to him. Before that icon, I begin and conclude the days, entrusting to the tenderness of Our Lady, who is Mother, all of you, your Church. It may be said that I begin and end the days "in Ukrainian," looking at Our Lady.

The main role of the Church, faced with the complex situations caused by the conflicts, is that of offering witness of *Christian hope*. Not a hope of the world, that is based on passing things, that come and go, and often divide, but the hope that never lets us down, that never gives way to discouragement, that knows how to overcome every tribulation with the gentle strength of the Spirit (see *Rom* 5: 2–5). Christian hope, nurtured by Christ's light, makes the resurrection and life shine even in the world's darkest nights. Therefore, dear Brothers, I hope that in difficult times, even more than in those of peace, the priority for believers may be that of remaining united to Jesus, our hope. It is about renewing that union based in Baptism and rooted in faith, rooted in the history of our communities, rooted in the great witnesses: I think of the line of everyday heroes, of those numerous "saints next door" who, with simplicity, in your people, responded to evil with good (see *Mt* 5:39–44). In the violent field of history they planted Christ's cross. And they bore fruit. These brothers and sisters of yours who suffered persecution and martyrdom and who, clinging only to the Lord Jesus, rejected the logic of the world, according to which one responds to violence with violence, wrote with their lives the clearest pages of the faith: they are fruitful seeds of Christian hope. I read with emotion the book *Persecuted for the Truth*. Behind those priests, bishops, nuns, there is the people of God, who carries forward all the population with faith and prayer.

A few years ago the Synod of Bishops of the Ukrainian Greek-Catholic Church adopted a pastoral program entitled *The living parish, place of encounter with the living Christ*. In some traditions, the expression "living parish" is rendered with the adjective "vibrant." Indeed, the encounter with Jesus, spiritual life, prayer that vibrates in the beauty of your liturgy, transmits that beautiful force of peace, that soothes wounds and infuses courage, but not aggression. When, like water that springs from a well, we draw from that spiritual vitality and transmit it, the Church becomes fruitful. She becomes the announcer of the Gospel of hope, teacher of that inner life that no other institution is able to offer.

Therefore, I wish to encourage you all, inasmuch as you are pastors of the Holy People of God, to have this primary concern in all your activities: *prayer, spiritual life*. It is the first occupation, no other goes before it. May all know and see that in your tradition, you are one Church that knows how to speak in spiritual and not worldly terms (see *1 Cor* 2: 13). Because every person who approaches the Church needs heaven on earth, nothing else. May the Lord grant us this grace and ensure we are all devoted to our sanctification and that of the faithful who are entrusted to us. In the night of conflict that you are experiencing, as in Gethsemane, the Lord asks His people to "keep watch and pray," not to defend themselves, nor to attack. But the disciples sleep instead of praying, and upon Judas' arrival they draw their sword. They had not prayed and they fell to the temptation, the temptation of worldliness: the violent weakness of the flesh prevailed over the meekness of the Spirit. Not weariness, not the sword, not flight (see *Mt* 26: 40, 52, 56), but prayer and the gift of self unto the end are the responses the Lord awaits from His people. Only these responses are Christian, and these alone will save from the worldly spiral of violence.

The Church is called to realize her pastoral mission with various means. After prayer comes *closeness*. That which the Lord had asked of His apostles that evening, to stay close to Him and to keep watch (cf. *Mk* 14: 34), today He asks of His pastors: to stay with the people, keeping watch beside those who pass through the night of pain. The closeness of pastors to the faithful is a channel that is built day by day, and which brings the living water of hope. It is built thus, encounter after encounter, with the priests who know and take to heart the concerns of the people, and the faithful who, through the care they receive, assimilate the proclamation of the Gospel that the pastors transmit. They do not understand if the pastors are intent only on *saying God*; they understand if they make the effort to *give God*: giving themselves, remaining close, witnesses of the God of hope made flesh to walk the paths of man. May the Church be the place where hope is drawn, where the door is always found open, where consolation and encouragement are received. Never closed to anyone, but with an open heart: never staying there looking at the clock, never sending away those who need to be listened to. We are servers of time. We live in time. Please, do not fall to the temptation of living as slaves to the clock! Time, not the clock.

Pastoral care consists first of all of the liturgy which, as the major archbishop has often highlighted, along with spirituality and catechesis constitutes an element that characterizes the identity of the Ukrainian Greek-Catholic Church. In a world "so often disfigured by selfishness and greed, the liturgy reveals the way to the harmony of the new man" (Saint John Paul II, Apostolic Letter *Orientale lumen*, 11): the way of charity, of unconditional love, by which every other activity must be routed, as it nurtures the fraternal bond between people, within and outside the community. With this spirit of closeness, in 2016 I promoted a humanitarian initiative, in which I invited the Churches in Europe to participate, to offer aid to those who had been directly affected by the conflict. I once again thank with all my heart those who contributed to the realization of this collection, both at an economic and also an organizational and technical level. I would like this first initiative, by now substantially concluded, to be followed by other special projects. Already in this meeting, some information can be provided. It is very important to be close to all and to be practical, also to avoid the danger that a grave situation of suffering ends up being forgotten. One cannot forget the brother who suffers, wherever he may be from. One cannot forget the brother who suffers.

I would like to add a third word to prayer and closeness, which is so familiar to you: *synodality*. Being Church is being a community that walks together. It is not enough to *have* a synod, you must *be* a synod. The Church needs intense internal sharing: a living dialogue between the Pastors and between the Pastors and the faithful. As an Eastern Catholic Church, you already have a marked synodal expression in your canonical order, which calls for frequent and regular recourse to the assemblies of the Synod of Bishops. But every day we must be a synod, striving to walk together, not only with those who think in the same way—this would be easy—but with all believers in Jesus.

Three aspects revive synodality. First of all, *listening*: listening to the experiences and suggestions of the bishops and priests. It is important that everyone within the Synod feels they are heard. Listening is all the more important as you rise in the hierarchy. Listening is sensitivity and openness to the opinions of brothers, even those who are younger, even those who are considered less experienced. A second aspect: *co-responsibility*. We cannot be indifferent to the errors or the carelessness of others, without intervening in a fraternal but convinced way: our confreres need our thoughts, our encouragement, as well as our corrections, because, precisely, we are called to *walk together*. You cannot hide what is wrong and move on as if nothing had happened to defend your good name at all costs: charity must always be lived in truth, in transparency, in that *parrhesia* that purifies the Church and keeps it going. Synodality—third aspect—also means involvement of the laity: as full members of the Church, they too are called to express themselves, to give suggestions. Participants of ecclesial life, they should not only be welcomed but listened to. And I emphasize this verb: to listen. Whoever listens can then speak well. Those who are used to not listening, do not speak: they bark.

Synodality also leads to broadening horizons, to living the wealth of one's own tradition within the universality of the Church: to deriving benefits from good relations with other rites; to considering the beauty of sharing significant parts of one's theological and liturgical treasure with other communities, also not Catholic; to weaving fruitful relationships with other particular Churches, as well as with the Dicasteries of the Roman Curia. The unity in the Church will be far more fruitful, the more the understanding and cohesion between the Holy See and the particular Churches will be real. More precisely: the greater the understanding and cohesion between all the bishops and the bishop of Rome. This certainly "must not imply a diminished awareness of their own authenticity and originality" (*Orientale lumen*, 21), but rather form it within our Catholic, that is, universal, identity. Inasmuch as it is universal, it is endangered and can be worn away by attachment to particularisms of various types: ecclesial particularisms, nationalistic particularisms, political particularisms.

Dear brothers, may these two days of meetings, which I strongly desired, be strong moments of sharing, of mutual listening, of free dialogue, always inspired by the search for good, in the spirit of the Gospel. May they help us to walk better together. It is, in a certain sense, a sort of Synod dedicated to the themes that are most at the heart of the Ukrainian Greek-Catholic Church in this period, afflicted by the military conflict still underway and characterized by a series of political and ecclesial processes that are much broader than those regarding our Catholic Church. But I recommend to you this spirit, this discernment by which to confirm oneself: prayer and spiritual life in the first place; then closeness, especially to those who suffer; then synodality, walking together, an open journey, step by step, with meekness and obedience. I thank you, I accompany you on this journey and I ask you, please, to remember me in your prayers.

Thank you!

Canon Law Is Essential to Ecumenical Dialogue

Address to Participants in the Conference Promoted by the Society for the Law of the Eastern Churches

September 19, 2019

Dear Brothers and Sisters, Good Morning,

I offer my cordial greeting to all of you, professors of canon law, experts and members of the Society for the Law of the Eastern Churches, and to your President, whom I thank for her words. I congratulate you on the fiftieth anniversary of the Society, founded here in Rome in 1969, soon after the Second Vatican Council. . . .

Canon law is essential for ecumenical dialogue. Many of the theological dialogues pursued by the Catholic Church, especially with the Orthodox Church and the Oriental Churches, are of an ecclesiological nature. They have a canonical dimension too, since ecclesiology finds expression in the institutions and the law of the Churches. It is clear, therefore, that canon law is not only an aid to ecumenical dialogue, but also an essential dimension. Then too it is clear that ecumenical dialogue also enriches canon law.

I would like to offer the example of *synodality*. When translated into established institutions and procedures of the Church, synodality expresses the ecumenical dimension of canon law. On the one hand, we have the opportunity to learn from the synodal experience of other traditions, especially those of the Eastern Churches (cf. *Evangelii Gaudium*, 246). On the other hand, it is clear that the way in which the Catholic Church experiences synodality is important for its relations with other Christians. This is a challenge for ecumenism. Indeed, "the commitment to build a synodal Church—a mission to which we are all called, each with the role entrusted him by the Lord—has significant ecumenical implications" (*Address during the Ceremony Commemorating the Fiftieth Anniversary of the Institution of the Synod of Bishops*, 17 October 2015).

Based on the common canonical heritage of the first millennium, the current theological dialogue between the Catholic Church and the Orthodox Church seeks precisely a common understanding of primacy and synodality and their relationship in the service of the unity of the Church.

Dear friends, your research also has a synodal dimension: you walk together and, in mutual listening, evaluate your traditions and experiences to find ways to full unity. I am grateful for your work which, I am certain, will be of great help not only for the development of canon law but for our moving ever closer to the fulfilment of the Lord's prayer: "that they may all be one; [. . .] so that the world may believe" (*Jn* 17:21).

Invoking God's blessing upon your Society, I entrust all of you to the Blessed Virgin Mary that she may watch over you with her maternal affection. I assure you of my prayers, and I ask you also to pray for me. Thank you!

A Gift to Become Gifts

Homily, Holy Mass for the Opening of the Synod of Bishops for the Pan-Amazon Region

Saint Peter's Basilica, October 6, 2019

The Apostle Paul, the greatest missionary in the Church's history, helps us to make this "synod," this "journey together." His words to Timothy seem addressed to us, as pastors in the service of God's People.

Paul first tells Timothy: "I remind you to rekindle the gift of God that is within you through the laying on of my hands" (*2 Tim* 1:6). We are bishops because we have received a *gift of God*. We did not sign an agreement; we were not handed an employment contract. Rather, hands were laid on our heads so that we in turn might be hands raised to intercede before the Father, helping hands extended to our brothers and sisters. We received a gift so that we might become a gift. Gifts are not bought, traded or sold; they are received and given away. If we hold on to them, if we make ourselves the center and not the gift we have received, we become bureaucrats, not shepherds. We turn the gift into a job and its gratuitousness vanishes. We end up serving ourselves and using the Church.

Thanks to the gift we have received, our lives are directed to service. When the Gospel speaks of "useless servants" (*Lk* 17:10), it reminds us of this. The expression can also mean "unprofitable servants." In other words, we do not serve for the sake of personal profit or gain, but because we received freely and want to give freely in return (cf. *Mt* 10:8). Our joy will be entirely in serving, since we were first served by God, who became the servant of us all. Dear brothers, let us feel called here for service; let us put God's gift at the center.

To be *faithful* to our calling, our mission, Saint Paul reminds us that our gift has to be *rekindled*. The verb he uses in the original text is fascinating: *to rekindle*, literally, which means stoking a fire (*anazopyrein*). The gift we have received is a fire, a burning love for God and for our brothers and sisters. A fire does not burn by itself; it has to be fed or else it dies; it turns into ashes. If everything continues as it was, if we spend our days content that "this is the way things have always been done," then the gift vanishes, smothered by the ashes of fear and concern for defending the *status quo*. Yet "in no way can the Church restrict her pastoral work to the 'ordinary maintenance' of those who already know the Gospel of Christ. Missionary outreach is a clear sign of the maturity of an ecclesial community" (Benedict XVI, Apostolic Exhortation *Verbum Domini*, 95). For the Church is always on the move, always going out and never withdrawn into itself. Jesus did not come to bring a gentle evening breeze, but to light a fire on the earth.

The fire that rekindles the gift is the Holy Spirit, the giver of gifts. So Saint Paul goes on to say: "Guard the truth that has been entrusted to you by the Holy Spirit" (*2 Tim* 1:14). And again: "God did not give us a spirit of timidity, but a spirit of power and love and prudence" (v. 7). Not a spirit of timidity, but of *prudence*. Someone may think that prudence is a virtue of the "customs house," that checks everything to ensure that there is no mistake. No, prudence is a Christian virtue; it is a virtue of life, and indeed the virtue of governance. And God has given us this spirit of prudence. Paul places prudence in opposition to timidity. What is this prudence of the Spirit? As the *Catechism* teaches, prudence "is not to be confused with timidity or fear"; rather, it is "the virtue that disposes practical reason to discern our true good in every circumstance and to choose the right means of achieving it" (No. 1806).

Prudence is not indecision; it is not a defensive attitude. It is the virtue of the pastor who, in order to serve with wisdom, is able to discern, to be receptive to the newness of the Spirit. Rekindling our gift in the fire of the Spirit is the opposite of letting things take their course without doing anything. Fidelity to the newness of the Spirit is a grace that we must ask for in prayer. May the Spirit, who makes all things new, give us his own *daring prudence*; may he inspire our Synod to renew the paths of the Church in Amazonia, so that the fire of mission will continue to burn.

As we see from the story of the burning bush, God's fire burns, yet does not consume (cf. *Ex* 3:2). It is the fire of love that illumines, warms and gives life, not a fire that blazes up and devours. When peoples and cultures are devoured without love and without respect, it is not God's fire but that of the world. Yet how many times has God's gift been imposed, not offered; how many times has there been colonization rather than evangelization! May God preserve us from the greed of new forms of colonialism. The fire set by interests that destroy, like the fire that recently devastated Amazonia, is not the fire of the Gospel. The fire of God is warmth that attracts and gathers into unity. It is fed by sharing, not by profits. The fire that destroys, on the other hand, blazes up when people want to promote only their own ideas, form their own group, wipe out differences in the attempt to make everyone and everything uniform.

To rekindle the gift; to welcome the bold prudence of the Spirit; to be faithful to his newness. Saint Paul now moves on to a final exhortation: "Do not be ashamed then of testifying to our Lord, but take your share of suffering for the Gospel in the power of God" (*2 Tim* 1:8). Paul asks Timothy to bear witness to the Gospel, to suffer for the Gospel, in a word, to *live* for the Gospel. The proclamation of the Gospel is the chief criterion of the Church's life, it is her mission, her identity. A little later, Paul will write: "I am already on the point of being sacrificed" (4:6). To preach the Gospel is to live as an offering, to bear witness to the end, to become all things to all people (cf. *1 Cor* 9:22), to love even to the point of martyrdom. I am grateful to God that in the College of Cardinals there are some brother Cardinals who are martyrs, because they have experienced in this life the cross of martyrdom. The Apostle makes it quite clear that the Gospel is not served by worldly power, but by the *power of God* alone: by persevering *in humble love*, by believing that the only real way to possess life is to lose it through love.

Dear brothers and sisters, together let us look to the crucified Jesus, to his heart pierced for our salvation. Let us begin there, the source of the gift that has given us birth. From that heart, the Spirit who renews has been poured forth (cf. *Jn* 19:30). Let each and every one of us, then, feel called to give life. So many of our brothers and sisters in Amazonia are bearing heavy crosses and awaiting the liberating consolation of the Gospel, the Church's caress of love. So many of our brothers and sisters in Amazonia have given their lives. I would like to repeat here the words of our beloved Cardinal Hummes: when he arrives in those little towns of Amazonia, he goes to the cemetery to visit the tombs of missionaries. It is a gesture on the Church's behalf for those who gave their lives in Amazonia. And then, with a little shrewdness, he says to the Pope: "May they not be forgotten. They deserved to be canonized." For them and for all those who have given their lives and those who are still giving their lives, and with them, let us journey together.

The Four Dimensions of the Synod for Amazonia

Opening of the Special Assembly of the Synod of Bishops for the Pan-Amazon Region

October 7, 2019

Sisters and Brothers, Good Morning!

Welcome to all and thank you for your preparatory work: everyone has worked so hard, from that moment in Puerto Maldonado until today. Thank you very much.

The Synod for the Amazon, we might say that it covers four dimensions: the pastoral dimension, the cultural dimension, the social dimension, and the ecological dimension. The first, the pastoral dimension, is the essential one, the one that encompasses everything. Let us address it with a Christian heart and look at the reality of the Amazon with the eyes of disciples in order to comprehend it and interpret it with the eyes of disciples, because there are no neutral hermeneutics, aseptic hermeneutics; they are always conditioned by a prior option; our prior option is that of disciples. And the eyes of missionaries, because the love that the Holy Spirit has placed in us urges us to proclaim Jesus Christ, a proclamation—as we all know—that is not to be confused with proselytism. Let us try to face the reality of the Amazon with this pastoral heart, with the eyes of disciples and of missionaries, because that is what impels us to proclaim the Lord. And let us also approach the Amazonian peoples on tip-toe, respecting their history, their cultures, their good way of living in the etymological sense of the word, not in the social sense which we often attribute to them, because peoples have a proper identity, all peoples have their wisdom, a self-awareness; peoples have a way of feeling, a way of seeing reality, a history, a hermeneutic, and they tend to be protagonists of their history with these matters, with these qualities. And as outsiders we consider ideological colonizations that destroy or diminish the characteristics of the peoples. Ideological colonization is very widespread. And without any entrepreneurial apprehension, we consider offering them prepackaged programs, in order to "discipline" the Amazonian peoples, to discipline their history, their culture; or this concern to "domesticate" the indigenous peoples. When the Church has forgotten this, that is, the way she should approach a people, she has not been inculturated; she has actually come to disdain certain peoples. And how many failures we regret today. Let us think of [Roberto] de Nobili in India, of [Matteo] Ricci in China and so many others. The "homogenizing" and "homogenative" centralism has not allowed the peoples' authenticity to emerge.

Ideologies are dangerous weapons; we always have the tendency to latch on to an ideology in order to interpret a people. Ideologies are reductive and lead us to exaggeration in our claim to comprehend intellectually, but without accepting, comprehending without admiring, comprehending without assimilating. So reality is understood in categories, and the more common ones are the categories of "-isms." Thus, when we have to approach the reality of a certain indigenous people, we speak of indigenisms, and when we wish to propose a way to a better life, we do not ask them about it; we talk about developmentalism. These "-isms" reformulate life starting from the illuminated and the illuminist laboratory.

They are slogans that are taking root, and they set the approach to indigenous peoples. In our country, a slogan—"civility and barbarity"—served to divide, to destroy, and it reached its climax toward the end of the 1980s, destroying most of the indigenous peoples, because they were "barbarians," and "civility" came from the other side. It is the contempt for peoples,—and I take this experience from my land; this "civility and barbarity," which served to destroy peoples, still continues today in my homeland, with offensive words, and so we speak of second-tier forms of civility, those that come from barbarity; and today there are the "*bolitas, los paraguayanos, los paraguas, los cabecitas negras,*" always this distancing from the reality of a people, qualifying them and holding them at a distance. This is the experience in my country.

And then contempt. Yesterday I was very displeased to hear—in here—a sarcastic comment about that pious man who brought offerings with a feathered headdress. Tell me: what difference is there between wearing a feathered headdress and the tricorn hat worn by some officials of our dicasteries? So we run the risk of simply proposing pragmatic measures, when on the contrary a contemplation of the peoples is required, a capacity for admiration, which leads to thinking in a paradigmatic way. If someone comes with pragmatic intentions, pray the 'I am a sinner,' so that you may convert and open your heart toward a paradigmatic perspective that springs from the reality of the peoples.

We did not come here to invent social development programs or museum-type cultural preservation, nor for pastoral actions with the same non-contemplative manner by which actions of the opposite kind are moving forward: deforestation, uniformizing, exploitation. They also create programs that do not respect the poetry—if I may say so—, the reality of the peoples, which is sovereign. We must also guard against worldliness in how we solicit points of view, changes in organization. Worldliness always seeps in and distances us from the poetry of the peoples.

We have come here to contemplate, to comprehend, to serve the peoples. And we do so by taking a synodal path; we do so as a synod, not at round tables, not in conferences and further discussions: we do so as a synod, because a synod is not a parliament; it is not a parlor; it is not demonstrating who has more power in the media and who has more power on the web, in order to impose some idea or some plan. This would amount to a congregationalist Church, if we mean taking polls to find out who has the majority. Or a sensationalist Church so far off, so distant from our Blessed Mother, the Catholic Church, or as Saint Ignatius loved to say: "our Blessed Mother the hierarchical Church." Synod means walking together under the inspiration and guidance of the Holy Spirit.

The Holy Spirit is the primary actor of the synod. Please let us not drive him from the hall. Consultations have taken place; it has been discussed in the Episcopal Conferences, in the Pre-Synod Council; the *Instrumentum Laboris* has been developed, which as you know is a martyr-text, destined to be destroyed, because it is a point of departure for what the Spirit will do within us. And now let us walk under the guidance of the Holy Spirit. Now we must allow the Holy Spirit to express himself in this Assembly, to express himself among us, to express himself with us, through us, to express himself "despite" us, despite our resistance, which is normal that there be, because thus is the life of a Christian.

Therefore, what will our work be here, in order to ensure that this presence of the Holy Spirit may be fruitful? First and foremost, pray. Sisters and brothers, I ask you to pray a great deal. Reflect, dialogue, listen with humility, knowing that I do not know everything. And speak with courage, with *parrhesia*, even if I am embarrassed to do so, to say what I feel, to discern, and all this in here, safeguarding the fraternity that must exist herein, in order to favor this approach of reflection, prayer, discernment, of listening with humility, and speaking out with courage. After four interventions we shall have four minutes of silence. Someone said, "It is risky, Father, because they will fall asleep." During the Synod on young people, where we did the same thing, instead the opposite happened: they tended to fall asleep during the interventions—at least, during some—and woke up during the silence.

Lastly, being in synod means being encouraged to enter a process. It does not mean occupying space in the hall but to enter a process. And ecclesial processes have a need: they must be protected, cared for like a baby, supported at the beginning, cared for delicately. They need the warmth of the community; they need the warmth of Mother Church. This is how an ecclesial process grows. It is important to foster the attitude of respect, the fraternal atmosphere, the air of intimacy. It does not mean referring everything, as it comes. For it is not a matter of respect for those whom we must inform about a secret more proper to lodges than to the ecclesial community but of sensitivity and prudence in the communication that we must have with the outside. And this need to communicate to the many people outside who want to know, to our many brothers and sisters, journalists, who have the vocation to serve so that it may be broadcast, and to help them in this, press services, briefings, etc., will be provided.

But a process such as a synod can be somewhat ruined if, when I exit the hall, I can say what I think, voice my opinion. And then there will be that feature that I saw at several synods: that of the "inside synod" and the "outside synod." The inside synod which follows the journey of Mother Church, the synod of attention to processes; and the outside synod which, because information given with levity, communicated with imprudence, leads those who have the duty to inform, to misinform.

Thus, thank you for what you are doing. Thank you because you prayed for one another, and take courage. And, please, let us not lose our sense of humor. Thank you.

A Church with Open Doors

General Audience

October 23, 2019

Dear Brothers and Sisters, Good Morning!

The Book of the Acts of the Apostles recounts that after that transformative encounter with Jesus, Saint Paul is welcomed by the Church of Jerusalem thanks to the mediation of Barnabas, and he begins to proclaim Christ. However, due to the hostility of some, he is forced to move on to Tarsus, his native city, where Barnabas joins him in order to engage him in the long *journey of the Word of God*. We can say that the Book of the Acts of the Apostles on which we are commenting in these catecheses is the Book of the long journey of the Word of God: the Word of God is to be proclaimed, and to be proclaimed everywhere. This journey begins in the wake of severe persecution (cf. Acts 11:19); but instead of provoking a setback for evangelization, it becomes an opportunity to expand the field on which to sow the good seed of the Word. The Christians do not feel afraid. They must flee, but they flee with the Word and they spread the Word somewhat everywhere.

Paul and Barnabas arrive first in Antioch, Syria, where they stay for a whole year to teach and help the community to put down roots (cf. Acts 11:26). They proclaimed to the Hebrew community, to the Jews. Antioch thus becomes the center of missionary impulse, thanks to the preaching of the two evangelizers—Paul and Barnabas—which impresses the hearts of believers who, here in Antioch, are called "Christians" for the first time (cf. Acts 11:26).

The nature of the Church appears from the Book of Acts; she is not a fortress but a tent able to enlarge her space (cf. Is 54:2) and give access to all. Either the Church "goes forth" or she is not a Church; either she is on a journey always widening her space so that everyone can enter, or she is not a Church. A "Church whose doors are open" (Apostolic Exhortation *Evangelii Gaudium*, 46), always with open doors. When I see a small church here, in this city, or when I would see one in the other diocese that I come from, with closed doors, this is a bad sign. Churches should always have their doors open because this is the sign of what a church is: always open. The Church is always "called to be the house of the Father . . . so that if someone, moved by the Spirit, comes there looking for God, he or she will not find a closed door" (ibid., 47).

But this novelty of *doors open* to whom? To the *Gentiles,* because the Apostles were preaching to the Jews, but the Gentiles came to knock at the Church's doors; and this novelty of doors open to the Gentiles triggers a very lively controversy. Several Jews affirm the need to become Jewish through circumcision in order to be saved, and then to receive Baptism. They say: "Unless you are circumcised according to the custom of Moses, you cannot be saved" (Acts 15:1), that is, you cannot receive Baptism until afterwards. First the Jewish rite and then Baptism: this was their position. And to resolve the issue, Paul and Barnabas seek the advice of the Apostles and of the elders of Jerusalem, and what takes place is what is held to be the First Council in the history of the Church, *the Council or Assembly of Jerusalem*, to which Paul refers in the Letter to the Galatians (2:1–10).

A very delicate theological, spiritual and disciplinary issue is addressed, that is, *the relationship between faith in Christ and observance of the Law of Moses.* During the Assembly, the discourses of Peter and James—"pillars" of the Mother Church—are decisive (cf. Acts 15:7–21; Gal 2:9). They exhort not imposing circumcision on the Gentiles but, instead, asking them only to reject idolatry and all its expressions. From the discussion emerges the common path, and this decision was ratified with the so-called *Apostolic Letter* sent to Antioch.

The Assembly of Jerusalem sheds important light on the way to face differences and to seek the "truth in love" (Eph 4:15). It reminds us that the ecclesial method for resolving conflict is based on dialogue made of careful and patient listening and on discernment undertaken in the light of the Spirit. Indeed, it is the Spirit who helps to overcome closure and tension, and works within hearts so that they may achieve unity in truth and goodness. This text helps us understand synodality. It is interesting how they write the Letter: the Apostles begin by saying: "The Holy Spirit and we *believe* that. . . ." The presence of the Holy Spirit is proper to synodality, otherwise it is not synodality. It is the parlor, parliament, something else. . . .

Let us ask the Lord to strengthen in all Christians, particularly in presbyters, the desire and the responsibility of communion. May he help us to experience dialogue, listening and encounter with our brothers and sisters in faith and with those afar, in order to savor and manifest the fruitfulness of the Church which is called to be, in every age, the "joyous mother" of many children (cf. Ps 113[112]:9).

A Synod on Synodality

Closing of the Special Assembly of the Synod of Bishops for the Pan-Amazon Region

VATICAN BASILICA, OCTOBER 26, 2019

Firstly, I would like to thank you all for bearing witness by working, listening, researching, trying to put into practice this synodal spirit on which we are perhaps just learning to focus. And which we are still not able to finalize. But we are on the way; we are on a good path. We are increasingly coming to understand what this walking together is; we are beginning to understand what it means to discern, what it means to listen, what it means to incorporate the Church's rich tradition in cyclical moments. Some think that tradition is a museum of old things. I like to repeat what Gustav Mahler used to say: "Tradition is not the worship of ashes, but the preservation of fire." It is like a root from which comes sap, that makes the tree grow so that it bears fruit. To take this and make it move forward: this is what the first Fathers understood tradition to be. To receive and to walk in the same direction with this very beautiful three-fold dimension that Vincent of Lerins described back in the 5th century: Remaining absolutely intact and unaltered, Christian Dogma is consolidated with the years, more ample in the course of time, more exalted as it advances in age (cf. *Commonitorium*, Cap 23 : pl 50, 667–668). Thank you for all this.

One of the themes that were voted on and that obtained a majority—three themes obtained a majority for the next Synod—is that of synodality. I do not know whether it will be chosen; I have not decided yet. I am reflecting and thinking, but I can certainly say that we have journeyed a lot and we must still journey more along this path of synodality. Thank you all for your companionship.

The Post-Synodal Exhortation, which is not obligatory for the Pope to issue, probably not; excuse me, the easiest thing to do would be: "well, here is the document, you see to it." In any case, a word from the Pope on what he experienced during the Synod can do some good. I would like to say it before the end of the year so that not too much time goes by. Everything depends on the amount of time that I will have to think about it.

A Theology with the Breath of the Gospel

Address to Members of the International Theological Commission

NOVEMBER 29, 2019

Dear Brothers and Sisters, Good Morning!

I am pleased to meet you and I thank your president, Cardinal Ladaria, for the words he addressed to me on your behalf. You have reached the end of your ninth five-year period of work, but above all to an important anniversary, the fiftieth anniversary of the Commission: fifty years of service to the Church. I congratulate you on this Jubilee, which allows you to make grateful memory of your history.

As Benedict XVI recalled in his message, the Commission was inaugurated by Saint Paul VI as a fruit of the Second Vatican Council, to create a new bridge between theology and the Magisterium. From the beginning, eminent theologians have been members, contributing effectively to this end. This is borne out by the voluminous body of documents published: twenty-nine texts, points of reference for formation and theological reflection. In the last five years you have produced two relevant texts. The first offers a theological clarification on synodality in the life and mission of the Church. You have shown how the practice of synodality, traditional but always to be renewed, is the implementation, in the history of the People of God on their journey, of the Church as a mystery of communion, in the image of Trinitarian communion. As you know, this theme is very close to my heart: synodality is a style, it is walking together, and it is what the Lord expects of the

Church in the third millennium. And for this I thank you for your document, because today one thinks that synodality is taking each other by the hand and setting out on a journey, celebrating with the young, or carrying out an opinion poll: "What do you think about the priesthood for women?" That is mostly what is done, isn't it? Synodality is an ecclesial journey that has a soul, which is the Holy Spirit. Without the Holy Spirit there is no synodality. And you have done a good job to help in this. Thank you.

The second document proposes a discernment on the different interpretations of *religious freedom* today. If on the one hand there are those who still prevent it or openly oppose it, depriving the human being of an incomparable right, on the other hand, as you have stressed, the idea of an "ethically neutral" State circulates, which, in an ambiguous fluidity, also risks leading to an unjust marginalization of religions from civil life to the detriment of the common good. This is again the Enlightenment legacy in its new edition. Sincere respect for religious freedom, cultivated in a fruitful dialogue between the State and religions, and between the religions themselves, is instead a great contribution to the good of all and to peace. In addition to these two areas, you have reflected on *sacramentality* as the constitutive structure of the encounter between God and man, highlighting the need to overcome various forms of dissociation between faith and sacramental life.

The work and the way in which it was carried out correspond to the intention that fifty years ago presided over the creation of the Commission. At the suggestion of the first assembly of the Synod of Bishops, Saint Paul VI wanted to extend the fruitful collaboration between the Magisterium and theologians that had marked the Council meetings. He also wanted the diversity of cultures and ecclesial experiences to enrich the mission entrusted by the Holy See to the Congregation for the Doctrine of the Faith. Indeed, as theologians from various backgrounds and latitudes, you are mediators between faith and cultures, and in this way you take part in the essential mission of the Church: evangelization. You have a mission to generate the Gospel: you are called to bring the Gospel to light. Indeed, you are listening to what the Spirit is saying today to the Churches in different cultures in order to bring to light ever new aspects of the inexhaustible mystery of Christ, "in whom are hidden all the treasures of wisdom and knowledge" (*Col* 2: 3). And then help the first steps of the Gospel: prepare its ways, translating the faith for the man of today, so that each one can feel closer to and embraced by the Church, taken by the hand where he is, and accompanied to taste the sweetness of *kerygma* and its timeless novelty. Theology is called to this: it is not a professorial disquisition on life, but the incarnation of faith in life.

After fifty years of intense work there is still a long way to go, but in doing so the Commission will fulfill its vocation of also being a model and stimulus for those—laity and clergy, men and women—who wish to devote themselves to theology. Because only a beautiful theology, which has the breath of the Gospel and is not content to be merely functional, attracts. And to do theology well one must never forget its two constitutive dimensions. The first is *spiritual life*: only in humble and constant prayer, in openness to the Spirit, can one understand and translate the Word and do the will of the Father. Theology is born and grows on its knees! The second dimension is *ecclesial life*: to feel that one is in the Church and with the Church, in accordance with the formula of Saint Albert the Great: "*In dulcedine societatis, quaerere veritatem*" (in the sweetness of fraternity, seek the truth). Theology is not done as individuals, but in the community, at the service of all, to spread the good flavor of the Gospel to the brothers and sisters of our time, always with gentleness and respect.

And I would like to reaffirm, finally, something that I have said to you: the theologian must go ahead, must study what goes beyond; he must also face things that are not clear and risk in discussion. Among theologians, though. But he must give to the People of God the solid substance of faith, not feed the People of God with disputed questions. May the dimension of relativism, let's say, which will always be in discussion, remain between theologians—it is your vocation—but never take this to the people, because then the people lose their way and lose their faith. To the people, always the solid substance that feeds faith.

Fifty years: I reiterate my gratitude for what you do and for how you do it, and I hope that, with the help of Our Lady, Seat of Wisdom, you will continue your mission with joy.

An Ecclesial Dream

Post-Synodal Apostolic Exhortation
Querida Amazonia (Chapter 4: nns. 61–109)

February 2, 2020

The Church is called to journey alongside the people of the Amazon region. In Latin America, this journey found privileged expression at the Bishops' Conference in Medellín (1968) and its application to the Amazon region at Santarém (1972),[1] followed by Puebla (1979), Santo Domingo (1992) and Aparecida (2007). The journey continues, and missionary efforts, if they are to develop a Church with an Amazonian face, need to grow in a culture of encounter towards "a multifaceted harmony."[2] But for this incarnation of the Church and the Gospel to be possible, the great missionary proclamation must continue to resound.

The message that needs to be heard in the Amazon region

Recognizing the many problems and needs that cry out from the heart of the Amazon region, we can respond beginning with organizations, technical resources, opportunities for discussion and political programs: all these can be part of the solution. Yet as Christians, we cannot set aside the call to faith that we have received from the Gospel. In our desire to struggle side by side with everyone, we are not ashamed of Jesus Christ. Those who have encountered him, those who live as his friends and identify

---

[1]Cf. Documents of Santarém (1972) and Manaus (1997) in National Conference of the Bishops of Brazil, *Desafio missionário. Documentos da Igreja na Amazônia* (Brasilia, 2014), pp. 9–28 and 67–84.

[2]Cf. Apostolic Exhortation *Evangelii Gaudium* (24 November 2013), 220: AAS 105 (2013), 1110.

with his message, must inevitably speak of him and bring to others his offer of new life: "Woe to me if I do not preach the Gospel!" (*1 Cor* 9:16).

An authentic option for the poor and the abandoned, while motivating us to liberate them from material poverty and to defend their rights, also involves inviting them to a friendship with the Lord that can elevate and dignify them. How sad it would be if they were to receive from us a body of teachings or a moral code, but not the great message of salvation, the missionary appeal that speaks to the heart and gives meaning to everything else in life. Nor can we be content with a social message. If we devote our lives to their service, to working for the justice and dignity that they deserve, we cannot conceal the fact that we do so because we see Christ in them and because we acknowledge the immense dignity that they have received from God, the Father who loves them with boundless love.

They have a right to hear the Gospel, and above all that first proclamation, the *kerygma*, which is "the principal proclamation, the one which we must hear again and again in different ways, the one which we must announce one way or another."[3] It proclaims a God who infinitely loves every man and woman and has revealed this love fully in Jesus Christ, crucified for us and risen in our lives. I would ask that you re-read the brief summary of this "great message" found in Chapter Four of the Exhortation *Christus Vivit.* That message, expressed in a variety of ways, must constantly resound in the Amazon region. Without that impassioned proclamation, every ecclesial structure would become just another NGO and we would not follow the command given us by Christ: "Go into all the world and preach the Gospel to the whole creation" (*Mk* 16:15).

Any project for growth in the Christian life needs to be centered continually on this message, for "all Christian formation consists of entering more deeply into the kerygma."[4] The fundamental

---

[3]Ibid., 164: AAS 105 (2013), 1088–1089.
[4]Ibid., 165: AAS 105 (2013), 1089.

response to this message, when it leads to a personal encounter with the Lord, is fraternal charity, "the new commandment, the first and the greatest of the commandments, and the one that best identifies us as Christ's disciples."[5] Indeed, the kerygma and fraternal charity constitute the great synthesis of the whole content of the Gospel, to be proclaimed unceasingly in the Amazon region. That is what shaped the lives of the great evangelizers of Latin America, like Saint Turibius of Mogrovejo or Saint Joseph of Anchieta.

Inculturation

As she perseveres in the preaching of the kerygma, the Church also needs to grow in the Amazon region. In doing so, she constantly reshapes her identity through listening and dialogue with the people, the realities and the history of the lands in which she finds herself. In this way, she is able to engage increasingly in a necessary process of inculturation that rejects nothing of the goodness that already exists in Amazonian cultures, but brings it to fulfilment in the light of the Gospel.[6] Nor does she scorn the richness of Christian wisdom handed down through the centuries, presuming to ignore the history in which God has worked in many ways. For the Church has a varied face, "not only in terms of space . . . but also of time."[7] Here we see the authentic Tradition of the Church, which is not a static deposit or a museum piece, but the root of a constantly growing tree.[8] This millennial Tradition bears

---

[5]Ibid., 161: AAS 105 (2013), 1087.

[6]As the Second Vatican Council states in No. 44 of the Constitution *Gaudium et Spes*: "The Church learned early in her history to express the Christian message in the concepts and languages of different peoples and tried to clarify it in the light of the wisdom of their philosophers: it was an attempt to adapt the Gospel to the understanding of all and the requirements of the learned, insofar as this could be done. Indeed, this kind of adaptation and preaching of the revealed word must ever be the law of all evangelization. In this way it is possible to create in every country the possibility of expressing the message of Christ in suitable terms and to foster vital contact and exchange between the Church and different cultures."

[7]*Letter to the Pilgrim People of God in Germany*, 29 June 2019, 9.

[8]Cf. Saint Vincent of Lerins, *Commonitorium primum*, cap. 23: PL 50, 668: *"Ut annis scilicet consolidetur, dilatetur tempore, sublimetur aetate."*

witness to God's work in the midst of his people and "is called to keep the flame alive rather than to guard its ashes."[9]

Saint John Paul II taught that in proposing the Gospel message, "the Church does not intend to deny the autonomy of culture. On the contrary, she has the greatest respect for it," since culture "is not only an object of redemption and elevation but can also play a role of mediation and cooperation."[10] Addressing indigenous peoples of America, he reminded them that "a faith that does not become culture is a faith not fully accepted, not fully reflected upon, not faithfully lived."[11] Cultural challenges invite the Church to maintain "a watchful and critical attitude," while at the same time showing "confident attention."[12]

Here I would reiterate what I stated about inculturation in the Apostolic Exhortation *Evangelii Gaudium*, based on the conviction that "grace supposes culture, and God's gift becomes flesh in the culture of those who receive it."[13] We can see that it involves a double movement. On the one hand, a fruitful process takes place when the Gospel takes root in a given place, for "whenever a community receives the message of salvation, the Holy Spirit enriches its culture with the transforming power of the Gospel."[14] On the other hand, the Church herself undergoes a process of reception that enriches her with the fruits of what the Spirit has already mysteriously sown in that culture. In this way, "the Holy Spirit adorns the Church, showing her new aspects of revelation

---

[9] *Letter to the Pilgrim People of God in Germany*, 29 June 2019, 9. Cf. the words attributed to Gustav Mahler: "Tradition ist nicht die Anbetung der Asche, sondern die Weitergabe des Feuers": "Tradition is not the worship of ashes but the passing on of the flame."

[10] *Address to University Professors and Cultural Leaders*, Coimbra (15 May 1982): *Insegnamenti* 5/2 (1982), 1702–1703.

[11] *Message to the Indigenous Peoples of the American Continent*, Santo Domingo (12 October 1992), 6: *Insegnamenti* 15/2 (1992), 346; cf. *Address to Participants in the National Congress of the Ecclesial Movement of Cultural Commitment* (16 January 1982), 2: *Insegnamenti* 5/1 (1982), 131.

[12] Saint John Paul II, Post-Synodal Apostolic Exhortation *Vita Consecrata* (15 March 1996), 98: AAS 88 (1996), 474–475.

[13] No. 115: AAS 105 (2013), 1068.

[14] Ibid., 116: AAS 105 (2013), 1068.

and giving her a new face."[15] In the end, this means allowing and encouraging the inexhaustible riches of the Gospel to be preached "in categories proper to each culture, creating a new synthesis with that particular culture."[16]

"The history of the Church shows that Christianity does not have simply one cultural expression,"[17] and "we would not do justice to the logic of the incarnation if we thought of Christianity as monocultural and monotonous."[18] There is a risk that evangelizers who come to a particular area may think that they must not only communicate the Gospel but also the culture in which they grew up, failing to realize that it is not essential "to impose a specific cultural form, no matter how beautiful or ancient it may be."[19] What is needed is courageous openness to the novelty of the Spirit, who is always able to create something new with the inexhaustible riches of Jesus Christ. Indeed, "inculturation commits the Church to a difficult but necessary journey."[20] True, "this is always a slow process and that we can be overly fearful," ending up as "mere onlookers as the Church gradually stagnates."[21] But let us be fearless; let us not clip the wings of the Holy Spirit.

Paths of inculturation in the Amazon region

For the Church to achieve a renewed inculturation of the Gospel in the Amazon region, she needs to listen to its ancestral wisdom, listen once more to the voice of its elders, recognize the values present in the way of life of the original communities, and recover the rich stories of its peoples. In the Amazon region, we have inherited great riches from the pre-Columbian cultures. These

---

[15]Ibid.

[16]Ibid., 129: AAS 105 (2013), 1074.

[17]Ibid., 116: AAS 105 (2013), 1068.

[18]Ibid., 117: AAS 105 (2013), 1069.

[19]Ibid.

[20]Saint John Paul II, *Address to the Plenary Assembly of the Pontifical Council for Culture* (17 January 1987): *Insegnamenti* 10/1 (1987), 125.

[21]Apostolic Exhortation *Evangelii Gaudium* (24 November 2013), 129: AAS 105 (2013), 1074.

include "openness to the action of God, a sense of gratitude for the fruits of the earth, the sacred character of human life and esteem for the family, a sense of solidarity and shared responsibility in common work, the importance of worship, belief in a life beyond this earth, and many other values."[22]

In this regard, the indigenous peoples of the Amazon Region express the authentic quality of life as "good living." This involves personal, familial, communal and cosmic harmony and finds expression in a communitarian approach to existence, the ability to find joy and fulfillment in an austere and simple life, and a responsible care of nature that preserves resources for future generations. The aboriginal peoples give us the example of a joyful sobriety and in this sense, "they have much to teach us."[23] They know how to be content with little; they enjoy God's little gifts without accumulating great possessions; they do not destroy things needlessly; they care for ecosystems and they recognize that the earth, while serving as a generous source of support for their life, also has a maternal dimension that evokes respect and tender love. All these things should be valued and taken up in the process of evangelization.[24]

While working for them and with them, we are called "to be their friends, to listen to them, to speak for them and to embrace the mysterious wisdom which God wishes to share with us through them."[25] Those who live in cities need to appreciate this wisdom and to allow themselves to be "re-educated" in the face of frenzied consumerism and urban isolation. The Church herself can be a means of assisting this cultural retrieval through a precious synthesis with the preaching of the Gospel. She can also become

---

[22]Fourth General Meeting of the Latin American and Caribbean Episcopate, *Santo Domingo Document* (12–28 October 1992), 17.

[23]Apostolic Exhortation *Evangelii Gaudium* (24 November 2013), 198: AAS 105 (2013), 1103.

[24]Cf. Vittorio Messori, Joseph Ratzinger, *Rapporto sulla fede*, Cinisello Balsamo, 1985, 211–212.

[25]Apostolic Exhortation *Evangelii Gaudium* (24 November 2013), 198: AAS 105 (2013), 1103.

a sign and means of charity, inasmuch as urban communities must be missionary not only to those in their midst but also to the poor who, driven by dire need, arrive from the interior and are welcomed. In the same way, these communities can stay close to young migrants and help them integrate into the city without falling prey to its networks of depravity. All these forms of ecclesial outreach, born of love, are valuable contributions to a process of inculturation.

Inculturation elevates and fulfills. Certainly, we should esteem the indigenous mysticism that sees the interconnection and interdependence of the whole of creation, the mysticism of gratuitousness that loves life as a gift, the mysticism of a sacred wonder before nature and all its forms of life.

At the same time, though, we are called to turn this relationship with God present in the cosmos into an increasingly personal relationship with a "Thou" who sustains our lives and wants to give them a meaning, a "Thou" who knows us and loves us:

> "Shadows float from me, dead wood
> But the star is born without reproach
> over the expert hands of this child,
> that conquer the waters and the night.
> It has to be enough for me to know
> that you know me
> completely, from before my days."[26]

Similarly, a relationship with Jesus Christ, true God and true man, liberator and redeemer, is not inimical to the markedly cosmic worldview that characterizes the indigenous peoples, since he is also the Risen Lord who permeates all things.[27] In Christian experience,

---

[26]Pedro Casaldáliga, "Carta de navegar (*Por el Tocantins amazónico*)" in *El tiempo y la espera*, Santander, 1986.

[27]Saint Thomas Aquinas explains it in this way: "The threefold way that God is in things: one is common, by essence, presence and power; another by grace in his saints; a third in Christ, by union" (*Ad Colossenses*, II, 2).

"all the creatures of the material universe find their true meaning in the incarnate Word, for the Son of God has incorporated in his person part of the material world, planting in it a seed of definitive transformation."[28] He is present in a glorious and mysterious way in the river, the trees, the fish and the wind, as the Lord who reigns in creation without ever losing his transfigured wounds, while in the Eucharist he takes up the elements of this world and confers on all things the meaning of the paschal gift.

Social and spiritual inculturation

Given the situation of poverty and neglect experienced by so many inhabitants of the Amazon region, inculturation will necessarily have a markedly social cast, accompanied by a resolute defense of human rights; in this way it will reveal the face of Christ, who "wished with special tenderness to be identified with the weak and the poor."[29] Indeed, "from the heart of the Gospel we see the profound connection between evangelization and human advancement."[30] For Christian communities, this entails a clear commitment to the justice of God's kingdom through work for the advancement of those who have been "discarded." It follows that a suitable training of pastoral workers in the Church's social doctrine is most important.

At the same time, the inculturation of the Gospel in the Amazon region must better integrate the social and the spiritual, so that the poor do not have to look outside the Church for a spirituality that responds to their deepest yearnings. This does not mean an alienating and individualistic religiosity that would silence social demands for a more dignified life, but neither does it mean ignoring the transcendent and spiritual dimension, as if material development alone were sufficient for human beings. We are thus

---

[28]Encyclical Letter *Laudato Si'* (24 May 2015), 235: AAS 107 (2015), 939.

[29]Third General Meeting of the Latin American and Caribbean Episcopate, *Puebla Document* (23 March 1979), 196.

[30]Apostolic Exhortation *Evangelii Gaudium* (24 November 2013), 178: AAS 105 (2013), 1094.

called not merely to join those two things, but to connect them at a deeper level. In this way, we will reveal the true beauty of the Gospel, which fully humanizes, integrally dignifies persons and peoples, and brings fulfilment to every heart and the whole of life.

Starting points for an Amazonian holiness

This will give rise to witnesses of holiness with an Amazonian face, not imitations of models imported from other places. A holiness born of encounter and engagement, contemplation and service, receptive solitude and life in community, cheerful sobriety and the struggle for justice. A holiness attained by "each individual in his or her own way,"[31] but also by peoples, where grace becomes incarnate and shines forth with distinctive features. Let us imagine a holiness with Amazonian features, called to challenge the universal Church.

A process of inculturation involving not only individuals but also peoples demands a respectful and understanding love for those peoples. This process has already begun in much of the Amazon region. More than forty years ago, the bishops of the Peruvian Amazon pointed out that in many of the groups present in that region, those to be evangelized, shaped by a varied and changing culture, have been "initially evangelized." As a result, they possess "certain features of popular Catholicism that, perhaps originally introduced by pastoral workers, are now something that the people have made their own, even changing their meaning and handing them down from generation to generation."[32] Let us not be quick to describe as superstition or paganism certain religious practices that arise spontaneously from the life of peoples. Rather, we ought to know how to distinguish the wheat growing alongside the tares,

[31]Second Vatican Ecumenical Council, Dogmatic Constitution on the Church *Lumen Gentium*, 11; cf. Apostolic Exhortation *Gaudete et Exsultate* (19 March 2018), 10–11.

[32]Apostolic Vicariates of the Peruvian Amazon, "Segunda asamblea episcopal regional de la selva," San Ramón-Perú (5 October 1973), in *Éxodo de la Iglesia en la Amazonia. Documentos pastorales de la Iglesia en la Amazonia peruana*, Iquitos, 1976, 121.

for "popular piety can enable us to see how the faith, once received, becomes embodied in a culture and is constantly passed on."[33]

It is possible to take up an indigenous symbol in some way, without necessarily considering it idolatry. A myth charged with spiritual meaning can be used to advantage and not always be considered a pagan error. Some religious festivals have a sacred meaning and are occasions for gathering and fraternity, albeit in need of a gradual process of purification or maturation. A missionary of souls will try to discover the legitimate needs and concerns that seek an outlet in at times imperfect, partial or mistaken religious expressions, and will attempt to respond to them with an inculturated spirituality.

Such a spirituality will certainly be centered on the one God and Lord, while at the same time be in contact with the daily needs of people who strive for a dignified life, who want to enjoy life's blessings, to find peace and harmony, to resolve family problems, to care for their illnesses, and to see their children grow up happy. The greatest danger would be to prevent them from encountering Christ by presenting him as an enemy of joy or as someone indifferent to human questions and difficulties.[34] Nowadays, it is essential to show that holiness takes nothing away from our "energy, vitality or joy."[35]

The inculturation of the liturgy

The inculturation of Christian spirituality in the cultures of the original peoples can benefit in a particular way from the sacraments, since they unite the divine and the cosmic, grace and creation. In the Amazon region, the sacraments should not be viewed in discontinuity from creation. They "are a privileged way in which nature is taken up by God to become a means of mediating super-

[33]Apostolic Exhortation *Evangelii Gaudium* (24 November 2013), 123: AAS 105 (2013), 1071.

[34]Cf. Apostolic Exhortation *Gaudete et Exsultate* (19 March 2018), 126–127.

[35]Ibid., 32.

natural life."[36] They are the fulfillment of creation, in which nature is elevated to become a locus and instrument of grace, enabling us "to embrace the world on a different plane."[37]

In the Eucharist, God, "in the culmination of the mystery of the Incarnation, chose to reach our intimate depths through a fragment of matter." The Eucharist "joins heaven and earth; it embraces and penetrates all creation."[38] For this reason, it can be a "motivation for our concerns for the environment, directing us to be stewards of all creation."[39] In this sense, "encountering God does not mean fleeing from this world or turning our back on nature."[40] It means that we can take up into the liturgy many elements proper to the experience of indigenous peoples in their contact with nature, and respect native forms of expression in song, dance, rituals, gestures and symbols. The Second Vatican Council called for this effort to inculturate the liturgy among indigenous peoples;[41] over fifty years have passed and we still have far to go along these lines.[42]

On Sunday, "Christian spirituality incorporates the value of relaxation and festivity. [Nowadays] we tend to demean contemplative rest as something unproductive and unnecessary, but this is to do away with the very thing which is most important about work: its meaning. We are called to include in our work a dimension of receptivity and gratuity."[43] Aboriginal peoples are familiar with this gratuity and this healthy contemplative leisure. Our celebrations should help them experience this in the Sunday liturgy and encounter the light of God's word and the Eucharist, which illumines our daily existence.

The sacraments reveal and communicate the God who is close

---

[36]Encyclical Letter *Laudato Si'* (24 May 2015), 235: AAS 107 (2015), 939.

[37]Ibid.

[38]Ibid., 236: AAS 107 (2015), 940.

[39]Ibid.

[40]Ibid., 235: AAS 107 (2015), 939.

[41]Cf. Constitution on the Sacred Liturgy *Sacrosanctum Concilium*, 37–40, 65, 77, 81.

[42]During the Synod, there was a proposal to develop an "Amazonian rite."

[43]Encyclical Letter *Laudato Si'* (24 May 2015), 237: AAS 107 (2015), 940.

and who comes with mercy to heal and strengthen his children. Consequently, they should be accessible, especially for the poor, and must never be refused for financial reasons. Nor is there room, in the presence of the poor and forgotten of the Amazon region, for a discipline that excludes and turns people away, for in that way they end up being discarded by a Church that has become a toll-house. Rather, "in such difficult situations of need, the Church must be particularly concerned to offer understanding, comfort and acceptance, rather than imposing straightaway a set of rules that only lead people to feel judged and abandoned by the very Mother called to show them God's mercy."[44] For the Church, mercy can become a mere sentimental catchword unless it finds concrete expression in her pastoral outreach.[45]

Inculturation of forms of ministry

Inculturation should also be increasingly reflected in an incarnate form of ecclesial organization and ministry. If we are to inculturate spirituality, holiness and the Gospel itself, how can we not consider an inculturation of the ways we structure and carry out ecclesial ministries? The pastoral presence of the Church in the Amazon region is uneven, due in part to the vast expanse of the territory, its many remote places, its broad cultural diversity, its grave social problems, and the preference of some peoples to live in isolation. We cannot remain unconcerned; a specific and courageous response is required of the Church.

Efforts need to be made to configure ministry in such a way that it is at the service of a more frequent celebration of the Eucharist, even in the remotest and most isolated communities. At Aparecida, all were asked to heed the lament of the many Amazonian communities "deprived of the Sunday Eucharist for long periods

[44] Apostolic Exhortation *Amoris Laetitia* (19 March 2016), 49: AAS 108 (2016), 331; cf. ibid., 305: AAS 108 (2016), 436–437.

[45] Cf. ibid., 296, 308: AAS 108 (2016), 430–431, 438.

of time."[46] There is also a need for ministers who can understand Amazonian sensibilities and cultures from within.

The way of shaping priestly life and ministry is not monolithic; it develops distinctive traits in different parts of the world. This is why it is important to determine what is most specific to a priest, what cannot be delegated. The answer lies in the sacrament of Holy Orders, which configures him to Christ the priest. The first conclusion, then, is that the exclusive character received in Holy Orders qualifies the priest alone to preside at the Eucharist.[47] That is his particular, principal and non-delegable function. There are those who think that what distinguishes the priest is power, the fact that he is the highest authority in the community. Yet Saint John Paul II explained that, although the priesthood is considered "hierarchical," this function is not meant to be superior to the others, but rather is "totally ordered to the holiness of Christ's members."[48] When the priest is said to be a sign of "Christ the head," this refers principally to the fact that Christ is the source of all grace: he is the head of the Church because "he has the power of pouring out grace upon all the members of the Church."[49]

The priest is a sign of that head and wellspring of grace above all when he celebrates the Eucharist, the source and summit of the entire Christian life.[50] That is his great power, a power that can only be received in the sacrament of Holy Orders. For this reason, only the priest can say: "This is *my* body." There are other words too, that he alone can speak: "I absolve you from your sins." Because sacramental forgiveness is at the service of a worthy celebration of

---

[46]Fifth General Conference of the Latin American and Caribbean Bishops' Conferences, *Aparecida Document*, 29 June 2007, 100 e.

[47]Cf. Congregation for the Doctrine of the Faith, Letter *Sacerdotium Ministeriale* to Bishops of the Catholic Church on certain questions concerning the minister of the Eucharist (6 August 1983): AAS 75 (1983), 1001–1009.

[48]Apostolic Letter *Mulieris Dignitatem* (15 August 1988), 27: AAS 80 (1988), 1718.

[49]Saint Thomas Aquinas, *Summa Theologiae* III, q. 8, a.1, resp.

[50]Cf. Second Vatican Ecumenical Council, Decree on the Ministry and Life of Priests *Presbyterorum Ordinis*, 5; Saint John Paul II, Encyclical Letter *Ecclesia de Eucharistia* (17 April 2003), 26: AAS 95 (2003), 448.

the Eucharist. These two sacraments lie at the heart of the priest's exclusive identity.[51]

In the specific circumstances of the Amazon region, particularly in its forests and more remote places, a way must be found to ensure this priestly ministry. The laity can proclaim God's word, teach, organize communities, celebrate certain sacraments, seek different ways to express popular devotion and develop the multitude of gifts that the Spirit pours out in their midst. But they need the celebration of the Eucharist because it "makes the Church."[52] We can even say that "no Christian community is built up which does not grow from and hinge on the celebration of the most holy Eucharist."[53] If we are truly convinced that this is the case, then every effort should be made to ensure that the Amazonian peoples do not lack this food of new life and the sacrament of forgiveness.

This urgent need leads me to urge all bishops, especially those in Latin America, not only to promote prayer for priestly vocations, but also to be more generous in encouraging those who display a missionary vocation to opt for the Amazon region.[54] At the same time, it is appropriate that the structure and content of both initial and ongoing priestly formation be thoroughly revised, so that priests can acquire the attitudes and abilities demanded by dialogue with Amazonian cultures. This formation must be preeminently pastoral and favor the development of priestly mercy.[55]

---

[51] It is also proper to the priest to administer the Anointing of the Sick, because it is intimately linked to the forgiveness of sins: "And if he has committed sins, he will be forgiven" (*Jas* 5:15).

[52] *Catechism of the Catholic Church*, 1396; Saint John Paul II, Encyclical Letter *Ecclesia de Eucharistia* (17 April 2003), 26: AAS 95 (2003), 451; cf. Henri de Lubac, *Meditation sur l'Église* (Paris, 1968), 101.

[53] Second Vatican Ecumenical Council, Decree on the Ministry and Life of Priests *Presbyterorum Ordinis*, 6.

[54] It is noteworthy that, in some countries of the Amazon Basin, more missionaries go to Europe or the United States than remain to assist their own Vicariates in the Amazon region.

[55] At the Synod, mention was also made of the lack of seminaries for the priestly formation of indigenous people.

Communities filled with life

The Eucharist is also the great sacrament that signifies and realizes the Church's *unity*.[56] It is celebrated "so that from being strangers, dispersed and indifferent to each another, we may become united, equals and friends."[57] The one who presides at the Eucharist must foster communion, which is not just any unity, but one that welcomes the abundant variety of gifts and charisms that the Spirit pours out upon the community.

The Eucharist, then, as source and summit, requires the development of that rich variety. Priests are necessary, but this does not mean that permanent deacons (of whom there should be many more in the Amazon region), religious women and lay persons cannot regularly assume important responsibilities for the growth of communities, and perform those functions ever more effectively with the aid of a suitable accompaniment.

Consequently, it is not simply a question of facilitating a greater presence of ordained ministers who can celebrate the Eucharist. That would be a very narrow aim, were we not also to strive to awaken new life in communities. We need to promote an encounter with God's word and growth in holiness through various kinds of lay service that call for a process of education—biblical, doctrinal, spiritual and practical—and a variety of programs of ongoing formation.

A Church of Amazonian features requires the stable presence of mature and lay leaders endowed with authority[58] and familiar with the languages, cultures, spiritual experience and communal way of life in the different places, but also open to the multiplicity of gifts that the Holy Spirit bestows on everyone. For wherever there is a particular need, he has already poured out the charisms that

---

[56]Cf. Second Vatican Ecumenical Council, Dogmatic Constitution on the Church *Lumen Gentium*, 3.

[57]Saint Paul VI, *Homily on the Solemnity of Corpus Christi*, 17 June 1965: *Insegnamenti* 3 (1965), 358.

[58]It is possible that, due to a lack of priests, a bishop can entrust "participation in the exercise of the pastoral care of a parish . . . to a deacon, to another person who is not a priest, or to a community of persons" (*Code of Canon Law*, 517 §2).

can meet it. This requires the Church to be open to the Spirit's boldness, to trust in, and concretely to permit, the growth of a specific ecclesial culture that is *distinctively lay.* The challenges in the Amazon region demand of the Church a special effort to be present at every level, and this can only be possible through the vigorous, broad and active involvement of the laity.

Many consecrated persons have devoted their energies and a good part of their lives in service to the Kingdom of God in Amazonia. The consecrated life, as capable of dialogue, synthesis, incarnation and prophecy, has a special place in this diverse and harmonious configuration of the Church in the Amazon region. But it needs a new impetus to inculturation, one that would combine creativity, missionary boldness, sensitivity and the strength typical of community life.

Base communities, when able to combine the defense of social rights with missionary proclamation and spirituality, have been authentic experiences of synodality in the Church's journey of evangelization in the Amazon region. In many cases they "have helped form Christians committed to their faith, disciples and missionaries of the Lord, as is attested by the generous commitment of so many of their members, even to the point of shedding their blood."[59]

I encourage the growth of the collaborative efforts being made through the Pan Amazonian Ecclesial Network and other associations to implement the proposal of Aparecida to "establish a collaborative ministry among the local churches of the various South American countries in the Amazon basin, with differentiated priorities."[60] This applies particularly to relations between Churches located on the borders between nations.

Finally, I would note that we cannot always plan projects with stable communities in mind, because the Amazonian region sees a great deal of internal mobility, constant and frequently

---

[59]Fifth General Conference of the Latin American and Caribbean Bishops' Conferences, *Aparecida Document*, 29 June 2007, 178.

[60]Ibid., 475.

pendular migration; "the region has effectively become a migration corridor."[61] "Transhumance in the Amazon has not been well understood or sufficiently examined from the pastoral standpoint."[62] Consequently, thought should be given to itinerant missionary teams and "support provided for the presence and mobility of consecrated men and women closest to those who are most impoverished and excluded."[63] This is also a challenge for our urban communities, which ought to come up with creative and generous ways, especially on the outskirts, to be close and welcoming to families and young people who arrive from the interior.

The strength and gift of women

In the Amazon region, there are communities that have long preserved and handed on the faith even though no priest has come their way, even for decades. This could happen because of the presence of strong and generous women who, undoubtedly called and prompted by the Holy Spirit, baptized, catechized, prayed and acted as missionaries. For centuries, women have kept the Church alive in those places through their remarkable devotion and deep faith. Some of them, speaking at the Synod, moved us profoundly by their testimony.

This summons us to broaden our vision, lest we restrict our understanding of the Church to her functional structures. Such a reductionism would lead us to believe that women would be granted a greater status and participation in the Church only if they were admitted to Holy Orders. But that approach would in fact narrow our vision; it would lead us to clericalize women, diminish the great value of what they have already accomplished, and subtly make their indispensable contribution less effective.

Jesus Christ appears as the Spouse of the community that celebrates the Eucharist through the figure of a man who presides

[61] *Instrumentum Laboris*, 65.
[62] Ibid., 63.
[63] Ibid., 129, d, 2.

as a sign of the one Priest. This dialogue between the Spouse and his Bride, which arises in adoration and sanctifies the community, should not trap us in partial conceptions of power in the Church. The Lord chose to reveal his power and his love through two human faces: the face of his divine Son made man and the face of a creature, a woman, Mary. Women make their contribution to the Church in a way that is properly theirs, by making present the tender strength of Mary, the Mother. As a result, we do not limit ourselves to a functional approach, but enter instead into the inmost structure of the Church. In this way, we will fundamentally realize why, without women, the Church breaks down, and how many communities in the Amazon would have collapsed, had women not been there to sustain them, keep them together and care for them. This shows the kind of power that is typically theirs.

We must keep encouraging those simple and straightforward gifts that enabled women in the Amazon region to play so active a role in society, even though communities now face many new and unprecedented threats. The present situation requires us to encourage the emergence of other forms of service and charisms that are proper to women and responsive to the specific needs of the peoples of the Amazon region at this moment in history.

In a synodal Church, those women who in fact have a central part to play in Amazonian communities should have access to positions, including ecclesial services, that do not entail Holy Orders and that can better signify the role that is theirs. Here it should be noted that these services entail stability, public recognition and a commission from the bishop. This would also allow women to have a real and effective impact on the organization, the most important decisions and the direction of communities, while continuing to do so in a way that reflects their womanhood.

Expanding horizons beyond conflicts

It often happens that in particular places pastoral workers envisage very different solutions to the problems they face, and consequently propose apparently opposed forms of ecclesial organization. When this occurs, it is probable that the real response to the challenges of evangelization lies in transcending the two approaches and finding other, better ways, perhaps not yet even imagined. Conflict is overcome at a higher level, where each group can join the other in a new reality, while remaining faithful to itself. Everything is resolved "on a higher plane and preserves what is valid and useful on both sides."[64] Otherwise, conflict traps us; "we lose our perspective, our horizons shrink and reality itself begins to fall apart."[65]

In no way does this mean relativizing problems, fleeing from them or letting things stay as they are. Authentic solutions are never found by dampening boldness, shirking concrete demands or assigning blame to others. On the contrary, solutions are found by "overflow," that is, by transcending the contraposition that limits our vision and recognizing a greater gift that God is offering. From that new gift, accepted with boldness and generosity, from that unexpected gift which awakens a new and greater creativity, there will pour forth as from an overflowing fountain the answers that contraposition did not allow us to see. In its earliest days, the Christian faith spread remarkably in accordance with this way of thinking, which enabled it, from its Jewish roots, to take shape in the Greco-Roman cultures, and in time to acquire distinctive forms. Similarly, in this historical moment, the Amazon region challenges us to transcend limited perspectives and "pragmatic" solutions mired in partial approaches, in order to seek paths of inculturation that are broader and bolder.

Ecumenical and interreligious coexistence

In an Amazonian region characterized by many religions, we believers need to find occasions to speak to one another and to act together for the common good and the promotion of the poor. This has nothing to do with watering down or concealing our deepest convictions when we encounter others who think differently than

[64]Apostolic Exhortation *Evangelii Gaudium* (24 November 2013), 228: AAS 105 (2013), 1113.

[65]Ibid., 226: AAS 105 (2013), 1112.

ourselves. If we believe that the Holy Spirit can work amid differences, then we will try to let ourselves be enriched by that insight, while embracing it from the core of our own convictions and our own identity. For the deeper, stronger and richer that identity is, the more we will be capable of enriching others with our own proper contribution.

We Catholics possess in sacred Scripture a treasure that other religions do not accept, even though at times they may read it with interest and even esteem some of its teachings. We attempt to do something similar with the sacred texts of other religions and religious communities, which contain "precepts and doctrines that . . . often reflect a ray of that truth which enlightens all men and women."[66] We also possess a great treasure in the seven sacraments, which some Christian communities do not accept in their totality or in the same sense. At the same time that we believe firmly in Jesus as the sole Redeemer of the world, we cultivate a deep devotion to his Mother. Even though we know that this is not the case with all Christian confessions, we feel it our duty to share with the Amazon region the treasure of that warm, maternal love which we ourselves have received. In fact, I will conclude this Exhortation with a few words addressed to Mary.

None of this needs to create enmity between us. In a true spirit of dialogue, we grow in our ability to grasp the significance of what others say and do, even if we cannot accept it as our own conviction. In this way, it becomes possible to be frank and open about our beliefs, while continuing to discuss, to seek points of contact, and above all, to work and struggle together for the good of the Amazon region. The strength of what unites all of us as Christians is supremely important. We can be so attentive to what divides us that at times we no longer appreciate or value what unites us. And what unites us is what lets us remain in this world without being swallowed up by its immanence, its spiritual emptiness, its complacent selfishness, its consumerist and self-destructive individualism.

[66]Second Vatican Ecumenical Council, Declaration on the Relation of the Church to Non-Christian Religions *Nostra Aetate*, 2.

All of us, as Christians, are united by faith in God, the Father who gives us life and loves us so greatly. We are united by faith in Jesus Christ, the one Savior, who set us free by his precious blood and his glorious resurrection. We are united by our desire for his word that guides our steps. We are united by the fire of the Spirit, who sends us forth on mission. We are united by the new commandment that Jesus left us, by the pursuit of the civilization of love and by passion for the kingdom that the Lord calls us to build with him. We are united by the struggle for peace and justice. We are united by the conviction that not everything ends with this life, but that we are called to the heavenly banquet, where God will wipe away every tear and take up all that we did for those who suffer.

All this unites us. How can we not struggle together? How can we not pray and work together, side by side, to defend the poor of the Amazon region, to show the sacred countenance of the Lord, and to care for his work of creation?

The Mission Is to Remember Jesus

Catechesis on Prayer, 16:
The Prayer of the Nascent Church
General Audience

November 25, 2020

Dear Brothers and Sisters Good Morning!

The Church's first steps in the world were interspersed with prayer. The apostolic writings and the great narration of the *Acts of the Apostles* give us the image of a Church on the move, an active Church which, however, finds the basis and impulse for missionary action while gathered in prayer. The image of the early Community of Jerusalem is the point of reference for every other Christian experience. Luke writes in the Book of Acts: "And they devoted themselves to the apostles' teaching and fellowship, to the breaking of bread and the prayers" (2:42). The community persevered in prayer.

We find here four essential characteristics of ecclesial life: listening to the apostles' teaching, first; second, the safeguarding of mutual communion; third, the breaking of the bread; and fourth, prayer. They remind us that the Church's existence has meaning if it remains firmly united to Christ, that is, in community, in his Word, in the Eucharist and in prayer. It is the way we unite ourselves to Christ. Preaching and catechesis bear witness to the words and actions of the Teacher; the constant quest for fraternal communion shields us from selfishness and particularisms; the breaking of the bread fulfills the sacrament of Jesus' presence among us. He will never be absent; it is really him in the Eucharist. He lives and walks with us. And lastly, prayer, which is the space of dialogue with the Father, through Christ in the Holy Spirit.

Everything in the Church that grows outside of these "coordinates" lacks a foundation. To discern a situation, we need to ask ourselves: in this situation, how are these four coordinates present—preaching, the constant search for fraternal communion, charity, the breaking of the bread (that is, Eucharistic life), and prayer. Any situation needs to be evaluated in the light of these four coordinates. Whatever is not part of these coordinates lacks ecclesiality; it is not ecclesial. It is God who creates the Church, not the clamor of works. The Church is not a market; the Church is not a group of businesspeople who go forward with a new business. The Church is the work of the Holy Spirit whom Jesus sent to us to gather us together. The Church is precisely the work of the Spirit in the Christian community, in the life of the community, in the Eucharist, in prayer . . . always. And everything that grows outside of these coordinates lacks a foundation; it is like a house built upon sand (cf. *Mt* 7:24–27). It is God who creates the Church, not the clamor of works. It is Jesus' word that fills our efforts with meaning. It is in humility that we build the future of the world.

At times, I feel tremendous sadness when I see a community that has good will, but takes the wrong path because it thinks that the Church is built up in meetings, as if it were a political party: the majority, the minority, what does this one think, that one, the other. . . . "This is like a Synod, the synodal path that we must take." I ask myself: "But where is the Holy Spirit there? Where is prayer? Where is communitarian love? Where is the Eucharist?" Without these four coordinates, the Church becomes a human society, a political party—majority, minority—changes are made as if it were a company, according to majority or minority . . . But the Holy Spirit is not there. And the presence of the Holy Spirit is precisely guaranteed by these four coordinates. To evaluate whether a situation is ecclesial or not ecclesial, let us ask ourselves whether these four coordinates are present: life in community, prayer, the Eucharist. . . [preaching] . . . How is life developing along these four coordinates? If this is lacking, the Holy Spirit is lacking, and if the Holy Spirit is lacking, we will be a beautiful humanitarian charitable organization, good, good . . . even an ecclesial party, let's put it that way. But it is not the Church. And this is why the Church cannot grow by these things: she does not grow through proselytism, as any other company, she grows by attraction. And who provokes attraction? The Holy Spirit. Let us never forget Benedict XVI's words: "The Church does not grow through proselytizing, she grows by attraction." If the Holy Spirit—who is the one who attracts [people] to Jesus—is lacking, the Church is not there. There might be a beautiful friendship club, good, with good intentions, but not the Church, not synodality.

In reading the Acts of the Apostles we then discover what a powerful driving force of evangelization the *prayer gatherings* can be, where those who participate actually experience Jesus' presence and are touched by the Spirit. The members of the first community—although this always applies, even to us today—sensed that the narrative of the encounter with Jesus did not stop at the moment of the Ascension, but continued in their life. In recounting what the Lord said and did—listening to the Word—in praying to enter into communion with him, everything became alive. Prayer infuses light and warmth: the gift of the Spirit endowed them with fervor.

In this regard, the *Catechism* contains a very substantial expression. It says this: "The Holy Spirit . . . keeps the memory of Christ alive in his Church at prayer, also leads her toward the fullness of truth, to the whole truth, and inspires new formulations expressing the unfathomable mystery of Christ at work in his Church's life, sacraments, and mission" (n. 2625). This is the Spirit's work in the Church: *making us remember Jesus.* Jesus himself said so: he will teach you and remind you. The mission is to *remember* Jesus, but not as a mnemonic exercise. Christians, walking on the paths of mission, remember Jesus while they make him present once more; and from him, from his Spirit, they receive the "push" to go, to proclaim, to serve. In prayer, Christians immerse themselves in the mystery of God who loves each person, that God who desires the Gospel to be preached to everyone. God is God for everyone, and in Jesus every wall of separation has definitively crumbled: as Saint Paul says, He is our peace, that is, he "who has made us both one" (*Eph* 2:14). Jesus created unity.

In this way the life of the early Church had the rhythm of a continuous succession of celebrations, convocations, times of both communitarian and personal prayer. And it is the Spirit who granted strength to the preachers who set out on the journey, and who, for love of Jesus, sailed the seas, faced dangers, subjected themselves to humiliation.

God gives love, God asks for love. This is the mystical root of the believer's entire life. In prayer, the first Christians, but we too who have come many centuries later, all live the same experience. The Spirit inspires everything. And every Christian who is not afraid to devote time to prayer can make his or her own the words of the Apostle Paul: "the life I now live in the flesh I live by faith in the Son of God, who loved me and gave himself for me" (*Gal* 2:20). Prayer makes you aware of this. Only in the silence of adoration do we experience the whole truth of these words. We must recapture this sense of adoration. To adore, to adore God, to adore Jesus, to adore the Spirit. The Father, the Son and the Spirit: to adore. In silence. The prayer of adoration is the prayer that makes us recognize God as the beginning and the end of all of History. And this prayer is the living flame of the Spirit that gives strength to witness and to mission. Thank you.

We Are Church All Together

Address to the Faithful of the Diocese of Rome

SEPTEMBER 18, 2021

Dear Brothers and Sisters,

As you are aware, we are about to begin a synodal process, a journey on which the whole Church will reflect on the theme: *Towards a Synodal Church: Communion, Participation, Mission*: those three pillars. Three phases are planned, and will take place between October 2021 and October 2023. This process was conceived as an exercise in mutual listening. I want to emphasize this. It is an exercise of mutual listening, conducted at all levels of the Church and involving the entire People of God. The Cardinal Vicar, the auxiliary bishops, priests, religious and laity have to listen to one another, and then to everyone else. Listening, speaking and listening. It is not about garnering opinions, not a survey, but a matter of listening to the Holy Spirit, as we read in the book of Revelation: "Whoever has ears should listen to what the Spirit says to the churches" (2:7). To have ears, to listen, is the first thing we need to do. To hear God's voice, to sense his presence, to witness his passage and his breath of life.

Thus the prophet Elijah came to realize that God is always a God of surprises, even in the way he passes by and makes himself felt: "A strong and heavy wind was rending the mountains and crushing rocks . . . but the Lord was not in the wind. After the wind, there was an earthquake—but the Lord was not in the earthquake. After the earthquake, there was fire—but the Lord was not in the fire. After the fire, there was a tiny whispering sound. When he heard this, Elijah hid his face in his cloak" (*1 Kg* 19:11–13).

That is how God speaks to us. We need to open our ears to hear that tiny whispering sound, the gentle breeze of God, which scholars also translate as "a quiet whisper" or "a small, still voice."

The first step of the process (October 2021–April 2022) will take place in each diocese. That is why I am here, as your bishop, for this moment of sharing, because it is very important that the Diocese of Rome be committed to this process. Wouldn't it look bad if the Pope's own diocese was not committed to this? Yes, it would look bad, for the Pope, but also for you!

Synodality is not a chapter in an ecclesiology textbook, much less a fad or a slogan to be bandied about in our meetings. Synodality is an expression of the Church's nature, her form, style and mission. We can talk about the Church as being "synodal," without reducing that word to yet another description or definition of the Church. I say this not as a theological opinion or even my own thinking, but based on what can be considered the first and most important "manual" of ecclesiology: the Acts of the Apostles.

The word "synod" says it all: it means "journeying together." The Book of Acts is the story of a journey that started in Jerusalem, passed through Samaria and Judea, then on to the regions of Syria, Asia Minor, Greece, ending up in Rome. A journey that reveals how God's word, and the people who heed and put their faith in that word, journey together. The word of God journeys with us. Everyone has a part to play; no one is a mere extra. This is important: everyone has a part to play. The Pope, the Cardinal Vicar and the auxiliary bishops are not more important than the others; no, all of us have a part to play and no one can be considered simply as an extra. At that time, the ministries were clearly seen as forms of service. Authority derived from listening to the voice of God and of the people, inseparably. This kept those who received it humble, serving the lowly with faith and love. Yet that story, that journey, was not merely geographical, it was also marked by a constant inner restlessness. This is essential: if Christians do not feel a deep inner restlessness, then something is missing. That inner restlessness is born of faith; it impels us to consider what it is best to do, what needs to be preserved or changed. History teaches us that it is not good for the Church to stand still (cf. *Evangelii Gaudium*, 23). Movement is the fruit of docility to the Holy Spirit, who directs this history, in which all have a part to play, in which all are restless, never standing still.

Peter and Paul were not just two individuals with their own personalities. They represent two visions within much broader horizons. They were capable of reassessing things in the light of events, witnesses of an impulse that led them to stop and think—that is another expression we should remember: to stop and think. An impulse that drove them to be daring, to question, to change their minds, to make mistakes and learn from those mistakes, but above all to hope in spite of every difficulty. They were disciples of the Holy Spirit, who showed them the geography of salvation, opening doors and windows, breaking down walls, shattering chains and opening frontiers. This may mean setting out, changing course, leaving behind certain ideas that hold us back and prevent us from setting out and walking together.

We can see the Spirit driving Peter to go to the house of Cornelius, the pagan centurion, despite his qualms. Remember: Peter had had a disturbing vision in which he was told to eat things he considered impure. He was troubled, despite the assurance that what God has made clean should no longer be considered impure. While he was trying to grasp the significance of this vision, some men sent by Cornelius arrived. Cornelius too had received a vision and a message. He was a pious Roman official, sympathetic to Judaism, but not enough to be fully Jewish or Christian; he would not have made it past a religious "customs office." Cornelius was a pagan, yet he was told that his prayers were heard by God and that he should send and ask Peter to come to his house. At this point, with Peter and his doubts, and Cornelius uncertain and confused, the Spirit overcomes Peter's resistance and opens a new chapter of missionary history. That is how the Spirit works. In the meeting between those two men, we hear one of the most beautiful phrases of Christianity. Cornelius meets Peter and falls at his feet, but Peter, picking him up, tells him: "Get up. I too am a man" (*Acts* 10:26). All of us can say the same thing: "I am a man, I am a woman; we are all human." This is something we should all say, bishops too, all of us: "Get up. I too am a man."

The text also says that Peter conversed with Cornelius (cf. v. 27). Christianity should always be human and accessible, reconciling differences and distances, turning them into familiarity and proximity. One of the ills of the Church, indeed a perversion, is the clericalism that detaches priests and bishops from people, making them officials, not pastors. Saint Paul VI liked to quote the words of Terence: "I am a man: I regard nothing human as foreign to me." The encounter between Peter and Cornelius resolved a problem; it helped bring about the decision to preach directly to the pagans, in the conviction that—as Peter put it—"God shows no partiality" (*Acts* 10:34). There can be no discrimination in the name of God. Discrimination is a sin among us too, whenever we start to say: "We are the pure, we are the elect, we belong to this movement that knows everything, we are . . ." No! We are the Church, all of us together.

You see, we cannot understand what it means to be "catholic" without thinking of this large, open and welcoming expanse. Being Church is a path to enter into this broad embrace of God. To return to the Acts of the Apostles, we see the emerging problem of how to organize the growing number of Christians, and particularly how to provide for the needs of the poor. Some were saying that their widows were being neglected. The solution was found by assembling the disciples and determining together that seven men would be appointed full time for *diakonia*, to serve the tables (*Acts* 6:1–7). In this way, though service, the Church advanced, journeyed together, was "synodal," accompanied by discernment, amid the felt needs and realities of life and in the power of the Spirit. The Spirit is always the great "protagonist" of the Church's life.

There was also the clash of differing visions and expectations. We need not be afraid when the same thing happens today. Would that we could argue like that! Arguments are a sign of docility and openness to the Spirit. Serious conflicts can also take place, as was the case with the issue of circumcision for pagan converts, which was settled with the deliberation of the so-called Council of Jerusalem, the first Council. Today too, there can be a rigid way of looking at things, one that restricts God's *makrothymía*, his patient, profound, broad and farsighted way of seeing things. God sees into the distance; God is not in a hurry. Rigidity is another perversion, a sin against the patience of God, a sin against God's sovereignty. Today too.

So it was back then. Some converts from Judaism, in their self-absorption, maintained that there could be no salvation without submission to the Law of Moses. In this way, they opposed Paul, who proclaimed salvation directly in the name of Jesus. This opposition would have compromised the reception of the new pagan converts. Paul and Barnabas were sent to Jerusalem, to the Apostles and the elders. It was not easy: in discussing this problem, the arguments appeared irreconcilable; they debated at length. It was a matter of recognizing God's freedom of action, that no obstacles could prevent him from touching the hearts of people of any moral or religious background. The situation was resolved when they accepted the evidence that "God, who knows the heart"—as a good "cardiologist"—was on the side of the pagans being admitted to salvation, since he "gave them the Holy Spirit just as he did to us" (*Acts* 15:8). In this way, respect was shown for the sensibilities of all and excesses were tempered. They learned from Peter's experience with Cornelius. Indeed, the final "document" presents the Spirit as the protagonist in the process of decision-making and reflects the wisdom that he is always capable of inspiring: "It seemed good to the Holy Spirit and to us not to place on you any burden beyond these necessary things" (*Acts* 15:28).

". . . and to us." In this Synod, we want to get to the point where we can say, "it seemed good to the Holy Spirit and to us," for, guided by the Holy Spirit, you will be in constant dialogue among yourselves, but also in dialogue with the Holy Spirit. Remember those words: "It seemed good to the Holy Spirit and to us not to place on you any burden . . ." "It seemed good to the Holy Spirit and to us." That is how you should try to discuss things at every stage of this synodal process. Without the Holy Spirit, this will be a kind of diocesan parliament, but not a Synod. We are not holding a diocesan parliament, examining this or that question, but making a journey of listening to one another and to the Holy Spirit, discussing yes, but discussing with the Holy Spirit, which is a way of praying.

"To the Holy Spirit and to us." Still, it is always tempting to do things on our own, in an "ecclesiology of substitution," which can take many forms. As if, once ascended to heaven, the Lord had left a void needing to be filled, and we ourselves have to fill it. No, the Lord has left us the Spirit! Jesus' words are very clear: "I will pray to the Father and he will give you another Paraclete, to stay with you forever . . . I will not leave you orphans" (*Jn* 14:16.18). In fulfilment of this promise, the Church is a sacrament, as we read in *Lumen Gentium*, 1: "The Church, in Christ, is like a sacrament—a sign and instrument of communion with God and of the unity of the whole human race." That sentence, which echoes the testimony of the Council of Jerusalem, contradicts those who would take God's place, presuming to shape the Church on the basis of their own cultural and historical convictions, forcing it to set up armed borders, toll booths, forms of spirituality that blaspheme the gratuitousness of God's involvement in our lives. When the Church is a witness, in word and deed, of God's unconditional love, of his welcoming embrace, she authentically expresses her catholicity. And she is impelled, from within and without, to be present in every time and place. That impulse and ability are the Spirit's gift: "You will receive power when the Holy Spirit comes upon you, and you will be my witnesses in Jerusalem, throughout Judea and Samaria, and to the ends of the earth" (*Acts* 1:8). To receive the power of the Holy Spirit to become witnesses: this is our path as Church, and we will be Church if we take this path.

Being a synodal Church means being a Church that is the sacrament of Christ's promise that the Spirit will always be with us. We show this by growing in our relationship with the Spirit and the world to come. There will always be disagreements, thank God, but solutions have to be sought by listening to God and to the ways he speaks in our midst. By praying and opening our eyes to everything around us; by practicing a life of fidelity to the

Gospel; by seeking answers in God's revelation through a pilgrim hermeneutic capable of persevering in the journey begun in the Acts of the Apostles. This is important: the way to understand and interpret is through a pilgrim hermeneutic, one that is always journeying. The journey that began after the Council? No. The journey that began with the first Apostles and has continued ever since. Once the Church stops, she is no longer Church, but a lovely pious association, for she keeps the Holy Spirit in a cage. A pilgrim hermeneutic capable of persevering in the journey begun in the Acts of the Apostles. Otherwise, the Holy Spirit would be demeaned. Gustav Mahler—as I have said on other occasions—once stated that fidelity to tradition does not consist in worshiping ashes but in keeping a fire burning. As you begin this synodal journey, I ask you: what are you more inclined to do: guard the ashes of the Church, in other words, your association or group, or keep the fire burning? Are you more inclined to worship what you cherish, and which keep you self-enclosed—"I belong to Peter, I belong to Paul, I belong to this association, you to that one, I am a priest, I am a bishop . . ."—or do you feel called to keep the fire of the Spirit burning? Mahler was a great composer, but those words showed that he was also a teacher of wisdom. *Dei Verbum* (no. 8), citing the Letter to the Hebrews, tells us that "God, who spoke in partial and various ways to our fathers (*Heb* 1:1), uninterruptedly converses with the bride of his beloved Son." Saint Vincent of Lérins aptly compared human growth to the development of the Church's Tradition, which is passed on from one generation to the next. He tells us that "the deposit of faith" cannot be preserved without making it advance in such a way as "to be consolidated by years, enlarged by time, refined by age" (*Commonitorium primum*, 23: *ut annis consolidetur, dilatetur tempore, sublimetur aetate*). This is how our own journey should be. For reality, including theology, is like water; unless it keeps flowing, it becomes stagnant and putrefies. A stagnant Church starts to decay.

You see, then, how our Tradition is like a mass of leavened dough; we can see it growing and in that growth is communion: journeying together brings about true communion. Here too, the Acts of the Apostles can help us by showing us that communion does not suppress differences. It is the wonder of Pentecost, where different languages are not obstacles; by the working of the Holy Spirit, "each one heard them speaking in his own language" (*Acts* 2:8). Feeling at home, different but together on the same journey. [Pardon me for speaking so long, but the Synod is a serious matter, and so I have felt free to speak at length . . .]

To return to the synodal process, the diocesan phase is very important, since it involves listening to all the baptized, the subject of the infallible *sensus fidei in credendo*. There is a certain resistance to moving beyond the image of a Church rigidly divided into leaders and followers, those who teach and those who are taught; we forget that God likes to overturn things: as Mary said, "he has thrown down the rulers from their thrones but lifted up the lowly" (*Lk* 1:52). Journeying together tends to be more horizontal than vertical; a synodal Church clears the horizon where Christ, our sun, rises, while erecting monuments to hierarchy covers it. Shepherds walk with their people: we shepherds walk with our people, at times in front, at times in the middle, at times behind. A good shepherd should move that way: in front to lead, in the middle to encourage and preserve the smell of the flock, and behind, since the people too have their own "sense of smell." They have a nose for finding new paths for the journey, or for finding the road when the way is lost. I want to emphasize this, also for the bishops and priests of the diocese. In this synodal process, they should ask: "Am I capable of walking, of moving, in front, in between and behind, or do I remain seated in my chair, with mitre and crozier?" Shepherds in the midst of the flock, yet remaining shepherds, not the flock. The flock knows we are shepherds, the flock knows the difference. In front to show the way, in the middle to sense how people feel, behind to help the stragglers, letting the people sniff out where the best pastures are found.

The *sensus fidei* gives everyone a share in the dignity of the prophetic office of Christ (cf. *Lumen Gentium*, 34–35), so that they can discern the paths of the Gospel in the present time. It is the "sense of smell" proper to the sheep, but let us be careful: in the history of salvation, we are all sheep with regard to the Shepherd who is the Lord. The image (of sheep) helps us understand the two dimensions that contribute to this "sense of smell." One is individual and the other communitarian: we are sheep, yet we are also members of the flock, which in this case means the Church. These days, in the Office of Readings, we are reading from Augustine's sermon on pastors, where he tells us, "With you I am a sheep; for you I am a shepherd." These two aspects, individual and ecclesial, are inseparable: there can be no *sensus fidei* without sharing in the life of the Church, which is more than mere Catholic activism; it must above all be that "sense" that is nourished by the "mind of Christ" (*Phil* 2:5).

The exercise of the *sensus fidei* cannot be reduced to the communication and comparison of our own opinions on this or that issue, or a single aspect of the Church's teaching or discipline. No, those are instruments, verbalizations, dogmatic or disciplinary statements. The idea of distinguishing between majorities and minorities must not prevail: that is what parliaments do. How many times have those who were "rejected" become "the cornerstone" (cf. *Ps* 118:22; *Mt* 21:42), while those who were "far away" have drawn "near" (*Eph* 2:13). The marginalized, the poor, the hopeless were chosen to be a sacrament of Christ (cf. *Mt* 25:31–46). The Church is like that. And whenever some groups wanted to stand out more, those groups always ended badly, even denying salvation, in heresies. We can think of the heresies that claimed to lead the Church forward, like Pelagianism, and then Jansenism. Every heresy ended badly. Gnosticism and Pelagianism are constant temptations for the Church. We are so rightly concerned for the dignity of our liturgical celebrations, but we can easily end up simply becoming complacent. Saint John Chrysostom warns us: "Do you want to honor the body of Christ? Do not allow it to be despised in its members, that is, in the poor who lack clothes to cover themselves. Do not honor him here in the church with rich fabrics while outside you neglect him when he is suffering from cold and naked. The one who said, "this is my body," confirming the fact with his word, also said, "you saw me hungry and you did not feed me" and, "whenever you failed to do these things to one of the least of these, you failed to do it to me" (*Homilies on the Gospel of Matthew*, 50, 3). You may say to me: "Father, what do you mean? Are the poor, the beggars, young drug addicts, all those people that society discards, part of the Synod too?"

Yes, dear friends. It is not me who is saying this, but the Lord. They too are part of the Church, and you will not properly celebrate the Synod unless you somehow make them part of it (in a way to be determined), or spend time with them, not only listening to what they have to say, but also feeling what they feel, listening to them even if they may insult you. The Synod is for everyone, and it is meant to include everyone. The Synod is also about discussing our problems, the problems I have as your Bishop, the problems that the auxiliary Bishops have, the problems that priests and laity have, the problems that groups and associations have. So many problems! Yet unless we include the "problem people" of society, those left out, we will never be able to deal with our own problems. This is important: that we let our own problems come out in the dialogue, without trying to hide them or justify them. Do not be afraid!

We should feel ourselves part of one great people which has received God's promises. Those promises speak of a future in which all are invited to partake of the banquet God has prepared for every people (cf. *Is* 25:6). Here I would note that even the notion "People of God" can be interpreted in a rigid and divisive way, in terms of exclusivity and privilege; that was the case with the notion of divine "election," which the prophets had to correct, showing how it should rightly be understood. Being God's people is not a privilege but a gift that we receive, not for ourselves but for everyone. The gift we receive is meant to be given in turn. That is what vocation is: a gift we receive for others, for everyone. A gift that is also a responsibility. The responsibility of witnessing by our deeds, not just our words, to God's wonderful works, which, once known, help people to acknowledge his existence and to receive his salvation. Election is a gift. The question is this: if I am a

Christian, if I believe in Christ, how do I give that gift to others? God's universal saving will is offered to history, to all humanity, through the incarnation of his Son, so that all men and women can become his children, brothers and sisters among themselves, thanks to the mediation of the Church. That is how universal reconciliation is accomplished between God and humanity, that unity of the whole human family, of which the Church is a sign and instrument (cf. *Lumen Gentium*, 1). In the period prior to the Second Vatican Council, thanks to the study of the Fathers of the Church, there was a renewed realization that the people of God are directed towards the coming of the Kingdom, towards the unity of the human family created and loved by God. The Church, as we know and experience her in the apostolic succession, should be conscious of her relationship to this universal divine election and carry out her mission in its light. In that same spirit, I wrote my encyclical *Fratelli Tutti*. As Saint Paul VI said, the Church is a teacher of humanity, and today she aims at becoming a school of fraternity.

Why do I say these things? Because in the synodal process, our listening must take into account the *sensus fidei,* but it must not neglect all those "intuitions" found where we would least expect them, "freewheeling," but no less important for that reason. The Holy Spirit in his freedom knows no boundaries or tests of admission. If the parish is to be a home to everyone in the neighborhood, and not a kind of exclusive club, please, let's keep the doors and windows open. Don't limit yourself to those who come to church or think as you do—they may be no more than 3, 4 or 5 percent. Let everyone come in . . . Go out and meet them, let them question you, let their questions become your questions. Journey together: the Spirit will lead you; trust in the Spirit. Do not be afraid to engage in dialogue and even to be taken aback by what you hear, for this is the dialogue of salvation.

Don't be disheartened; be prepared for surprises. In the book of Numbers (22:8ff.) we hear of a donkey who became a prophet of God. The Hebrews were about to end the long journey that led them to the promised land. Their passage through his territory frightened Balak, the king of Moab, who told Balaam, a seer, to stop them, in hopes of avoiding a war. Balaam, who was in his own way a believer, asked God what to do. God told him not to go along with the king, but since the king insisted, Balaam set out on a donkey to do as the king said. The donkey, however, turned aside from the road because it saw an angel with an unsheathed sword, representing the opposition of God. Balaam tugged at the reins and beat the donkey, but could not get it to return to the road. Finally, the donkey opened his mouth and spoke, the beginning of a dialogue that would open the seer's eyes and turn his mission of cursing and death into a mission of blessing and life.

This story teaches us to trust that the Spirit will always make his voice heard. Even a donkey can become the voice of God, can open our eyes and change our course when we go astray. If a donkey can do that, how much more can a baptized person, a priest, a bishop, a Pope do it? We need but rely on the Holy Spirit, who uses all of creation to speak to us: he only asks us to clean out our ears, to hear better.

I came here to encourage you to take this synodal process seriously and to tell you that the Holy Spirit needs you. It is true: the Holy Spirit needs us. Listen to him by listening to each other. Leave no one behind or excluded. It will be good for the Diocese of Rome and for the whole Church, which is not strengthened simply by reforming structures (that is the great illusion!) or by giving instructions, offering retreats and conferences, by issuing guidelines and programs. All those things are good, but as part of something else, namely our rediscovery that we are a people meant to walk together, with one another and with all humanity. A people that, here in Rome, embraces a wide variety of communities and situations: an extraordinary treasure, in all its complexity! However, we need to pass beyond the 3 or 4 percent that are closest to us, to broaden our range and to listen to others; at times they may insult or dismiss you, but we need to hear what they are thinking, without trying to impose our own concerns: let the Spirit speak to us.

In this time of pandemic, the Lord is guiding the Church's mission as a sacrament of care. Our world has cried out and shown its vulnerability: our world needs care.

Take heart and keep going! Thank you!

Three Keywords:
Communion, Participation, Mission

A Moment of Reflection
for the Beginning of the Synodal Path

October 9, 2021

Dear Brothers and Sisters,

Thank you for being here for the opening of the Synod. You have come by many different roads and from different Churches, each bearing your own questions and hopes. I am certain the Spirit will guide us and give us the grace to move forward together, to listen to one another and to embark on a discernment of the times in which we are living, in solidarity with the struggles and aspirations of all humanity. I want to say again that the Synod is not a parliament or an opinion poll; the Synod is an ecclesial event and its protagonist is the Holy Spirit. If the Spirit is not present, there will be no Synod.

May we experience this Synod in the spirit of Jesus' fervent prayer to the Father on behalf of his disciples: "that they may all be one" (*Jn* 17:21). This is what we are called to: unity, communion, the fraternity born of the realization that all of us are embraced by the one love of God. All of us, without distinction, and in particular those of us who are bishops. As Saint Cyprian wrote: "We must maintain and firmly uphold this unity, above all ourselves, the bishops who preside in the Church, in order to demonstrate that the episcopate is itself one and undivided" (*De Ecclesiae Catholicae Unitate*, 5). In the one People of God, therefore, let us journey together, in order to experience a Church that receives and lives this gift of unity, and is open to the voice of the Spirit.

The Synod has three key words: *communion, participation,* and *mission.* Communion and mission are theological terms describing the mystery of the Church, which we do well to keep in mind. The Second Vatican Council clearly taught that *communion* expresses the very nature of the Church, while pointing out that the Church has received "the *mission* of proclaiming and establishing among all peoples the kingdom of Christ and of God, and is, on earth, the seed and beginning of that kingdom" (*Lumen Gentium*, 5). With those two words, the Church contemplates and imitates the life of the Blessed Trinity, a mystery of communion *ad intra* and the source of mission *ad extra.* In the wake of the doctrinal, theological and pastoral reflections that were part of the reception of Vatican II, Saint Paul VI sought to distill in those two words—communion and mission—"the main lines enunciated by the Council." Commemorating the opening of the Council, he stated that its main lines were in fact "communion, that is, cohesion and interior fullness, in grace, truth and collaboration . . . and mission, that is, apostolic commitment to the world of today" (*Angelus* of 11 October 1970), which is not the same as proselytism.

In 1985, at the conclusion of the Synod marking the twentieth anniversary of the close of the Council, Saint John Paul II also reiterated that the Church's nature is *koinonia*, which gives rise to her mission of serving as a sign of the human family's intimate union with God. He went on to say: "It is most useful that the Church celebrate ordinary, and on occasion, also extraordinary synods." These, if they are to be fruitful, must be well prepared: "it is necessary that the local Churches work at their preparation with the participation of all" (*Address at the Conclusion of the II Extraordinary Assembly of the Synod of Bishops*, 7 December 1985). And this brings us to our third word: *participation.* The words "communion" and "mission" can risk remaining somewhat abstract, unless we cultivate an ecclesial praxis that expresses *the concreteness of synodality* at every step of our journey and activity, encouraging real involvement on the part of each and all. I would say that celebrating a Synod is always a good and important thing, but it proves truly beneficial if it becomes a living expression of "being

Church," of a way of acting marked by true participation.

This is not a matter of form, but of faith. Participation is a requirement of the faith received in baptism. As the Apostle Paul says, "in the one Spirit we were all baptized into one body" (*1 Cor* 12:13). In the Church, everything starts with baptism. Baptism, the source of our life, gives rise to the equal dignity of the children of God, albeit in the diversity of ministries and charisms. Consequently, all the baptized are called to take part in the Church's life and mission. Without real participation by the People of God, talk about communion risks remaining a devout wish. In this regard, we have taken some steps forward, but a certain difficulty remains and we must acknowledge the frustration and impatience felt by many pastoral workers, members of diocesan and parish consultative bodies and women, who frequently remain on the fringes. Enabling everyone to participate is an essential ecclesial duty! All the baptized, for baptism is our identity card.

The Synod, while offering a great opportunity for a pastoral conversion in terms of mission and ecumenism, is not exempt from *certain risks*. I will mention three of these. The first is *formalism*. The Synod could be reduced to an extraordinary event, but only externally; that would be like admiring the magnificent facade of a church without ever actually stepping inside. The Synod, on the other hand, is a process of authentic spiritual discernment that we undertake, not to project a good image of ourselves, but to cooperate more effectively with the work of God in history. If we want to speak of a synodal Church, we cannot remain satisfied with appearances alone; we need content, means and structures that can facilitate dialogue and interaction within the People of God, especially between priests and laity. Why do I insist on this? Because sometimes there can be a certain elitism in the presbyteral order that detaches it from the laity; the priest ultimately becomes more a "landlord" than a pastor of a whole community as it moves forward. This will require changing certain overly vertical, distorted and partial visions of the Church, the priestly ministry, the role of the laity, ecclesial responsibilities, roles of governance and so forth.

A second risk is *intellectualism*. Reality turns into abstraction and we, with our reflections, end up going in the opposite direction. This would turn the Synod into a kind of study group, offering learned but abstract approaches to the problems of the Church and the evils in our world. The usual people saying the usual things, without great depth or spiritual insight, and ending up along familiar and unfruitful ideological and partisan divides, far removed from the reality of the holy People of God and the concrete life of communities around the world.

Finally, the temptation of *complacency*—the attitude that says: "We have always done it this way" (*Evangelii Gaudium*, 33) and it is better not to change. That expression—"We have always done it that way"—is poison for the life of the Church. Those who think this way, perhaps without even realizing it, make the mistake of not taking seriously the times in which we are living. The danger, in the end, is to apply old solutions to new problems. A patch of rough cloth that ends up creating a worse tear (cf. *Mt* 9:16). It is important that the synodal process be exactly this: a process of becoming, a process that involves the local Churches, in different phases and from the bottom up, in an exciting and engaging effort that can forge a style of communion and participation directed to mission.

And so, brothers and sisters, let us experience this moment of encounter, listening and reflection as *a season of grace* that, in the joy of the Gospel, allows us to recognize at least *three opportunities*. First, that of moving *not occasionally but structurally* towards a *synodal Church*, an open square where all can feel at home and participate. The Synod then offers us the opportunity to become a *listening Church*, to break out of our routine and pause from our pastoral concerns in order to stop and listen. To listen to the Spirit in adoration and prayer. Today how much we miss the prayer of adoration; so many people have lost not only the habit but also the very notion of what it means to worship God! To listen to our brothers and sisters speak of their hopes and of the crises of faith present in different parts of the world, of the need for a renewed pastoral life and of the signals we are receiving from those on the ground. Finally, it offers us the opportunity to become a *Church of closeness*. Let us keep going back to God's own "style," which is closeness, compassion and tender love. God has always operated that way. If we do not become this Church of closeness with attitudes of compassion and tender love, we will not be the Lord's Church. Not only with words, but by a presence that can weave greater bonds of friendship with society and the world. A Church that does not stand aloof from life, but immerses herself in today's problems and needs, bandaging wounds and healing broken hearts with the balm of God. Let us not forget God's style, which must help us: closeness, compassion and tender love.

Dear brothers and sisters, may this Synod be a true season of the Spirit! For we need the Spirit, the ever new breath of God, who sets us free from every form of self-absorption, revives what is moribund, loosens shackles and spreads joy. The Holy Spirit guides us where God wants us to be, not to where our own ideas and personal tastes would lead us. Father [Yves] Congar, of blessed memory, once said: "There is no need to create *another Church*, but to create a *different Church*" (*True and False Reform in the Church*). That is the challenge. For a "different Church," a Church open to the newness that God wants to suggest, let us with greater fervor and frequency invoke the Holy Spirit and humbly listen to him, journeying together as he, the source of communion and mission, desires: with docility and courage.

Come, Holy Spirit! You inspire new tongues and place words of life on our lips: keep us from becoming a "museum Church," beautiful but mute, with much past and little future. Come among us, so that in this synodal experience we will not lose our enthusiasm, dilute the power of prophecy, or descend into useless and unproductive discussions. Come, Spirit of love, open our hearts to hear your voice! Come, Holy Spirit of holiness, renew the holy and faithful People of God! Come, Creator Spirit, renew the face of the earth! Amen.

Synod, Path of Spiritual and Ecclesial Discernment

Homily for the Holy Mass Opening of the Synodal Path

St Peter's Basilica, October 10, 2021

A certain rich man came up to Jesus "as he was setting out on his journey" (*Mk* 10:17). The Gospels frequently show us Jesus "on a journey"; he walks alongside people and listens to the questions and concerns lurking in their hearts. He shows us that God is not found in neat and orderly places, distant from reality, but walks ever at our side. He meets us where we are, on the often rocky roads of life. Today, as we begin this synodal process, let us begin by asking ourselves—all of us, Pope, bishops, priests, religious and laity—whether we, the Christian community, embody this "style" of God, who travels the paths of history and shares in the life of humanity. Are we prepared for the adventure of this journey? Or are we fearful of the unknown, preferring to take refuge in the usual excuses: "It's useless" or "We've always done it this way"?

Celebrating a Synod means walking on the same road, walking together. Let us look at Jesus. First, he *encounters* the rich man on the road; he then *listens* to his questions, and finally he helps him *discern* what he must do to inherit eternal life. *Encounter, listen and discern.* I would like to reflect on these three verbs that characterize the Synod.

The first is *encounter*. The Gospel passage begins by speaking of an encounter. A man comes up to Jesus and kneels down before him, asking him a crucial question: "Good Teacher, what must I do to inherit eternal life?" (v. 17). So important a question requires attention, time, willingness to encounter others and sensitivity to what troubles them. The Lord is not standing aloof; he does not appear annoyed or disturbed. Instead, he is completely present to this person. He is open to encounter. Nothing leaves Jesus indifferent; everything is of concern to him. Encountering faces, meeting eyes, sharing each individual's history. That is the closeness that Jesus embodies. He knows that someone's life can be changed by a single encounter. The Gospel is full of such encounters with Christ, encounters that uplift and bring healing. Jesus did not hurry along, or keep looking at his watch to get the meeting over. He was always at the service of the person he was with, listening to what he or she had to say.

As we initiate this process, we too are called to become experts in the *art of encounter*. Not so much by organizing events or theorizing about problems, as in taking time to encounter the Lord and one another. Time to devote to prayer and to adoration—that form of prayer that we so often neglect—devoting time to adoration, and to hearing what the Spirit wants to say to the Church. Time to look others in the eye and listen to what they have to say, to build rapport, to be sensitive to the questions of our sisters and brothers, to let ourselves be enriched by the variety of charisms, vocations and ministries. Every encounter—as we know—calls for openness, courage and a willingness to let ourselves be challenged by the presence and the stories of others. If at times we would rather take refuge in formality or presenting the proper image—the clerical and courtly spirit, where I am more *Monsieur l'abbé* than *Father*—the experience of encounter changes us; frequently it opens up new and unexpected possibilities. Following today's Angelus, I will meet with a group of street people who came together simply because a group of people made an effort to listen to them, sometimes just to listen to them. And from that listening they succeeded in setting out on a new path. So often God points out new paths in just this way. He invites us to leave our old habits behind. Everything changes once we are capable of genuine encounters with him and with one another, without formalism or pretense, but simply as we are.

The second verb is *listen*. True encounter arises only from listening. Jesus listened to that man's question and to the religious and existential concerns that lay behind it. He did not give a non-committal reply or offer a prepackaged solution; he did not pretend to respond politely, simply as a way of dismissing him and continuing on his way. Jesus simply listens, for whatever amount of time it takes; he is not rushed. Most importantly, he is not afraid *to listen to him with his heart* and not just with his ears. Indeed, he does more than simply answer the rich man's question; he lets him tell his story, to speak freely about himself. Christ reminds him of the commandments, and the man starts to talk about his youth, to share his religious journey and his efforts to seek God. This happens whenever we listen with the heart: people feel that they are being heard, not judged; they feel free to recount their own experiences and their spiritual journey.

Let us ask ourselves frankly during this synodal process: Are we good at listening? How good is the "hearing" of our heart? Do we allow people to express themselves, to walk in faith even though they have had difficulties in life, and to be part of the life of the community without being hindered, rejected or judged? Participating in a Synod means placing ourselves on the same path as the Word made flesh. It means following in his footsteps, listening to his word along with the words of others. It means discovering with amazement that the Holy Spirit always surprises us, to suggest fresh paths and new ways of speaking. It is a slow and perhaps tiring exercise, this learning to listen to one another—bishops, priests, religious and laity, all the baptized—and to avoid artificial and shallow and pre-packaged responses. The Spirit asks us to listen to the questions, concerns and hopes of every Church, people and nation. And to listen to the world, to the challenges and changes that it sets before us. Let us not soundproof our hearts; let us not remain barricaded in our certainties. So often our certainties can make us closed. Let us listen to one another.

Finally, *discern*. Encounter and listening are not ends in themselves, leaving everything just as it was before. On the contrary, whenever we enter into dialogue, we allow ourselves to be challenged, to advance on a journey. And in the end, we are no longer the same; we are changed. We see this in today's Gospel. Jesus senses that the person before him is a good and religious man, obedient to the commandments, but he wants to lead him beyond the mere observance of precepts. Through dialogue, he helps him to discern. Jesus encourages that man to look within, in the light of the love that the Lord himself had shown by his gaze (cf. v. 21), and to discern in that light what his heart truly treasures. And in this way to discover that he cannot attain happiness by filling his life with more religious observances, but by emptying himself, selling whatever takes up space in his heart, in order to make room for God.

Here is a valuable lesson also for us. The Synod is a process of spiritual discernment, of ecclesial discernment, that unfolds in adoration, in prayer and in dialogue with the word of God. Today's second reading tells us that God's word is "living and active, sharper than any two-edged sword, piercing to the division of soul and spirit, of joints and marrow, and discerning the thoughts and intentions of the heart" (*Heb* 4:12). That word summons us to discernment and it brings light to that process. It guides the Synod, preventing it from becoming a Church convention, a study group or a political gathering, a parliament, but rather a grace-filled event, a process of healing guided by the Spirit. In these days, Jesus calls us, as he did the rich man in the Gospel, to empty ourselves, to free ourselves from all that is worldly, including our inward-looking and outworn pastoral models; and to ask ourselves what it is that God wants to say to us in this time. And the direction in which he wants to lead us.

Dear brothers and sisters, let us have a good journey together! May we be pilgrims in love with the Gospel and open to the surprises of the Holy Spirit. Let us not miss out on the grace-filled opportunities born of encounter, listening and discernment. In the joyful conviction that, even as we seek the Lord, he always comes with his love to meet us first.